FREEDOM AND NECESSITY

FREEDOM AND NECESSITY

*An Introduction to
the Study of Society*

Joan Robinson

Where do correct ideas come from?
Do they drop from the skies? No. Are
they innate in the mind? No. They
come from social practice.

Mao Tse-tung

VINTAGE BOOKS
A Division of Random House, New York

FIRST VINTAGE BOOKS EDITION APRIL 1971

Library of Congress Catalog Card Number: 70-110126

MANUFACTURED IN THE UNITED STATES OF AMERICA

PREFACE

This book is intended to provoke inquiry rather than to give information. It seems to me that an economic interpretation of history is an indispensable element in the study of society, but it is only one element. In layers below it lie geography, biology and psychology, and in layers above it the investigation of social and political relationships and the history of culture, law and religion.

This book offers a hasty sketch of the central layer in the hope of providing a general framework within which specialist studies can be elaborated.

The time scheme is an inverted cone. Successive chapters cover aeons, then millenia, then centuries and decades. Then five chapters survey the contemporary scene. The last two chapters comment upon the teaching of social science.

For Chapter 1 I had invaluable criticism and advice from Professor Thorpe and from Mrs Alison Jolly. Chapter 2 owes a great deal to Professor George Dalton of Northwestern University; Edmund Leach, the Provost of King's College, and Professor Meyer Fortes headed me off from some errors, as did Professor Postan in later chapters. No doubt errors remain; in any case disputable views abound. Among contemporaries, I have drawn upon the ideas of the late Karl Polanyi, Ester Boserup, Barrington Moore, J. K. Galbraith and Gunnar Myrdal. These are all controversial writers; moreover they would not necessarily agree with me or support the use that I have made of their work. The student must not take anything here on faith. I offer only an angle of vision which I hope may illuminate his further inquiries.

Cambridge
June 1969

Joan Robinson

CONTENTS

I

THE ORIGIN OF SOCIETY

CONSIDER the profiles of a dolphin and a herring. The resemblance between them consists in each being well suited to swimming. The evolutionary relationship between them is extremely remote. Presumably the lineage of the dolphin branched off from that of the fish in the palaeozoic age and in due course took to warm-blooded life on land. Returning to the water, the limbs of the dolphin's ancestors became fins and the chunky profile of a quadruped became streamlined. In the fish and the dolphin, the same technical situation – the requirements of aquatic life – produced similar results, though working upon very different material.

There are many examples of this process in the similarities between animals in Australia and in other continents. Isolated in Australia, the marsupials evolved a highly diversified set of species including mice, rats, anteaters, wolves and many more, each closely resembling the creature that goes by the same name among placental animals and adapted to profit by similar food supplies. (Australia, however, produced also a type of its own, presumably because in arid land the only large animal that could survive had to have a wide range and capacity to travel fast.)

The plasticity which makes adaption possible does not depend mainly upon mutations in the genes which control heredity. (These are more often harmful than helpful to the species.) With sexual reproduction, the same stock of genes is passed on with continual permutations and combinations which produce minor variations in each brood or litter of young. Most species produce a number of young every year, while for a stable population (where the sex ratio is one to one) each female must be survived by two over a lifetime. The survivors of each generation are those whose genetic make-up is propitious to survival, that is, well suited to finding nourishment and avoiding enemies in the particular environment in which they grow up. Thus the pressure of technical conditions has carved out the multiplicity of creatures who appear to us to be so marvellously 'designed' for the life that they lead.[1]

For a species, variability itself is propitious, within limits, to survival. The species capable of adaptation are, for the most part, the ones that have survived till today, though there are some which have proved successful with remarkably little variation.

The habits of a species are just as much subject to the pressure of evolution as its physical form. A great variety of types of family life exist in nature – monogamy, polygamy, and group marriage; continuous association, pairing during a limited breeding season or casual mating. The style of life of a species must be consonant with its way of getting a living. Thus, where the food supply is dispersed and requires skill to find or catch, the family unit consists of a pair looking after the young until they disperse to fend for themselves. The robin redbreast and the lion provide familiar examples. Where the food supply is more or less evenly spread over large areas, a gregarious style of life is possible; the herbivores of the prairies generally live in herds; feeding upon plankton permits group life for whales.

The problem of survival is not only to eat but also to avoid being eaten. Animals whose defence against predators is in hiding, nocturnal habits, or protective colouring are generally solitary. Birds that flock in winter, when they can rely upon flight, disperse to settle for nesting. The herds upon the plains cannot conceal themselves and rely upon group precautions or group defence. The great colonies of

[1] Cf. Sir Alistair Hardy, *The Living Stream*. Here this view is put forward as though it were heretical, but nowadays it seems to be generally accepted.

sea-birds of many kinds illustrate both principles at once, for they have a plentiful food supply and safe cliffs or islands on which to breed.[2]

For a species to be viable, its habits of life must fit its habitat, but there is an element in the mechanism of evolution which to some extent cuts across purely economic pressure; that is, sexual selection. In some species, particularly those which are polygamous, there is competition between males to get the most mates and to stimulate them most effectively. This gives survival value to gorgeous plumage which, however, is dangerously conspicuous, or an elaborate apparatus for ritual fights, such as the antlers of stags, which are useless for defence and put an extra burden on the needs of the individual for nourishment. Economic necessity, so to say, contains such extravagances and keeps them within bounds, for a species that went further in this direction than its environment permits would wipe itself out.

The most striking example of the principle that resemblances between species result from the pressure of circumstances rather than heredity is the fact that some of the closest analogies with human society are found amongst ants.[3] They have specialized professions; some keep domestic animals to supply food; some capture the young of allied species and bring them up as slaves to work for them; amongst these, some of the master races have become degenerate and entirely dependent for life upon their slaves; in some, wars break out between settlements of the same species when they find themselves in each other's way, a phenomenon which is unknown amongst other animals except rats and men. Clearly this has nothing to do with inheritance. The evolutionary relationship between ants and men is even more remote than that between fishes and dolphins.

[2] This line of thought was suggested to me by Alison Jolly.
[3] See C. P. Haskins, *Of Ants and Men*, Chapters VIII and IX.

Still less is there any reason to suppose that ants have
subjective experiences that resemble those of which we are
conscious in ourselves. But amongst warm-blooded animals
and perhaps even among some fishes, it seems that the
habits which survival requires are controlled by an
apparatus of emotions. It is hardly likely that there will
ever be any possibility of finding direct evidence of the
subjective consciousness of another being, but even the
strictest philosophical solipsist in daily life goes upon the
assumption that other people have feelings. At one time,
to attribute feelings to animals was considered sentimental
and unscientific, but now the tide has turned and it is
considered more sentimental to suppose that man is in every
way totally different from his fellow mortals.[4]

To regard our own feelings as rooted in a biologically
determined apparatus requires a certain degree of detach-
ment. Take the example of hunger. We think that we desire
to eat because food is necessary to life, but it is by no means
so simple. We desire to eat because we are endowed with
an apparatus that makes us feel hungry, and we are
endowed with that apparatus because a species that lacked
it would not have survived. In some illnesses the patient
suffers a total absence of appetite; then to push external
substances inside oneself seems not merely boring but
actually abhorrent. An intellectual perception that food is
necessary for life is not enough to get it down.

The connection of the survival of a species with sexual
attraction and maternal devotion is perhaps more obvious.
Even in this respect the similarities between humans and
other species have been, so to say, moulded afresh by the
requirements of survival, not directly inherited. Thus, in
many human societies family life is organized around
possessiveness and male jealousy. This can be observed
amongst the birds in any garden. It has been fully described

[4] Cf. W. H. Thorpe, 'Ethnology and Consciousness' in *Brain and
Conscious Experience*, ed. John C. Eccles.

by Lorenz among grey-lag geese.[5] But our cousins the chimpanzees are apparently immune from it.[6]

In the matter of habits, pressure upon the individual to conform to specifications is less strict than in the matter of physique. For Lorenz's geese the standard pattern is life-long monogamy, but few couples were found to conform to it – which led to the remark: After all, geese are only human![7] Sometimes, apparently by accident, a couple of two ganders was formed. Being stronger and more impressive than a normal pair of goose and gander, these couples flourished. From the point of view of their individual life they were a success, but a species in which this happened too often would die out.

Some degree of variation amongst individuals is not merely tolerable but actually advantageous for the species, for useful habits can be pioneered by nonconformist individuals.

In each group, some are more adventurous than others, bolder, more curious. Trying this and that, some particular genius finds out, say, a new source of nourishment and the discovery is disseminated by imitation. This must often have happened within historic times, as when sea-gulls first learned to follow the plough for worms or to look out for promising donors of bread in London parks. One example of it has occured very recently. Since milk bottles capped with tin foil or cardboard began to be left on doorsteps, tits have found out how to drink cream. (The first recorded observation in England was in 1921; in Holland the habit died out during the war for lack of milk bottles and sprang up again after 1948.) It seems that, in a number of separate localities, particular individuals discovered the milk bottles as a source of an agreeable article of diet, sometimes a few years after they first began to be available. From a number

[5] Lorenz, *Aggression*. See Chapter XI.

[6] See Verun and Francis Reynolds in *Primate Behaviour*, Editor Irven DeVore, p. 420.

[7] Lorenz, loc. cit., p. 167.

of independent centres the habit spread out in widening circles, presumably by the broad masses imitating the pioneers in each neighbourhood, and passing on the new lore from one generation to the next.[8]

The spread of a kind of drug addiction is seen in the case of English greenfinches. They feed upon the berries of an ornamental garden shrub which have an intoxicating effect. The habit is believed to have been started by a single pioneer in the Midlands. It has been spreading north and south, at the rate of a few kilometres a year, for more than a century.[9]

Though birds seem to have an apparatus of emotions which resemble our own, and although episodes such as learning to rob milk bottles might appear at first glance to imply insight into the nature of a problem, the conceptual apparatus of birds is very different from ours. They are equipped to respond to particular stimuli, not to analyse a situation. Thus, a bunch of red feathers on a stick will call out from a robin all the hostility appropriate to a rival male. When milk bottles with different-coloured caps were in use, tits in various suburbs specialized on one or other particular colour (the one, presumably, that the pioneer in each district first happened upon) and ignored bottles with caps of other colours that were standing on the same doorsteps. This seems to rule out insight as an element in this type of discovery. Rather the process consists in trial and error, the propensity to make new trials being strong in a small proportion of the population and the capacity to imitate successful trials being general.

Originality and individualism are useful to the species provided there is not too much of them. For the most part,

[8] See James Fisher and R. A. Hinde, 'The Opening of Milk Bottles by Birds' *British Birds*, Vol. XLII, November 1949, and 'Further Observations' on the same subject, Vol. XLIX, December 1951.

[9] See W. H. Thorpe, *Learning and Instinct in Animals* (1963), pp. 355–6.

conformity with the pattern of habits that has been proved viable must be imposed upon all. For this reason, a long helpless infancy, which in itself makes a species vulnerable, indirectly led to social life and a system for learning correct behaviour, which made a great leap forward in the process of evolution. The marsupials had much less need for it than the placentals. For them, mother and child are an independent unit; until a great age, joey can climb back into the pouch for safety. Moreover, Australia did not produce any large carnivore till man came on the scene, so that the struggle for survival was weaker than in other continents.

With placental birth and several years of growth to maturity, group life became necessary. In some species the group is a 'nuclear family' of a pair with their young, in others a large herd or troupe of many families.

'Why does the group exist? Why does the animal not live alone, if not all year at least for much of it? There are many reasons but the principal one is learning. The group is the locus of knowledge and experience far exceeding that of the individual member. It is in the group that experience is pooled and the generations linked. The adaptive function of prolonged biological youth is that it gives the animal time to learn. During this period, while the animal learns from other members of the group, it is protected by them. Slow development in isolation would simply mean disaster for the individual and extinction for the species.

* * *

'To emphasize the importance of learned behaviour in no way minimizes the importance of biology. Indeed, learning can profitably be viewed in the adaptive context of evolutionary biology. The biology of a species expresses itself through behaviour, and limits what can be learned. Evolution, through selection, has built the biological base so that many behaviours are easily, almost inevitably learned.'[10]

The Indian elephant evidently has a higher level of social development and problem-solving intelligence than, say, the lemurs. But in lemurs evolution had introduced stereoscopic vision and a pair of hands. It was the development of intelligence in this physique that proved to be the way forward. The lemurs appear to have a highly developed emotional apparatus which provides the basis for social life in large groups, but they could not compete with the intelligent monkeys; they are now living only on the island of Madagascar, which monkeys did not invade.[11]

The economic life of each species consists in the adjustment of population to food supply. This is often secured by the establishment of property in a territory. The territory is defended by the family or group against others of the same species, but not against members of other species whose diet is different.[12] By this means each species is spread out over all the region that is habitable for it and each family commands its means of livelihood. This mechanism operates for many kinds of birds and mammals, even for insects. It provides clear evidence of adaptation to the technical necessities of life, rather than of a common inheritance. It is very strictly enforced, for instance, by robins all the year round,[13] by many other birds only in the breeding season. Where food is plentiful and enemies rare, as for instance for gorillas, conceptions of territory are quite vague.[14]

Methods of defending a territory are very various. The

[10] Sherwood L. Washburn and David A. Hamburg, in *Primate Behaviour*, p. 613; see also p. 620.

[11] See Alison Jolly, *Lemur Behaviour*.

[12] S. L. Washburn and D. A. Hamburg, in *Primate Behaviour*, p. 615.

[13] David Lack, *The Life of the Robin*.

[14] Washburn and Hamburg, loc. cit.

robin establishes his claim by singing, and furiously attacks a red-breasted intruder. The howler monkeys challenge a threatened invasion to a shouting match, lemurs to a stinking match. In every case there is a kind of ritual character in the fight. The home side always wins and the invaders admit defeat. A species which fought to the death would be in danger of wiping itself out.

Once the habitable region has been fully populated, there must be some mechanism to keep numbers in check. A species which increased without limit would sooner or later destroy its food supply and would fall a victim to famine and internecine strife. But before it becomes cataclysmic, scarcity of food checks breeding and increases infant mortality. Moreover as a species grows, it provides more plentiful diet for its predators, so that the 'balance of nature' is preserved. It has been noticed that amongst lions, who have few powerful enemies, the jealousy of the father checks the cubs from eating so that only a few of the strongest grow up. Amongst some kinds of alligators, the newly hatched young are a favourite diet of the male.

Amongst social animals it appears that territory is not of merely economic importance :

'The adaptive advantages of living in a known area may be shown by the case of a baboon that changed groups. Both the groups involved had been studied prior to the change and the baboon was known as an adult male that had been living on the edge of one troop. There were five male adults that dominated him and drove him to the periphery of the group whenever he tried to enter it. He shifted to the next group and defeated the only adult male in it. Here, then, he was the number-one adult male in dominance, but in a new group. The group into which he had moved ranged in the park beside Victoria Falls. It was possibly the tamest troop in Africa and its members were completely used to human beings. The new dominant male was afraid of humans, hid behind bushes, and dared not take the food that the rest of the group was getting. As time went on he learned which humans to avoid, how to steal mangoes, and which paths to take. Six weeks later, when the study ended, this male was still learning the behaviour appropriate to the group in which he was the most dominant male.

'Range is the economic base, but to exploit the range the group must learn the local conditions, the dangers and the opportunities. Although local adaptation through learning is emphasized here, it must be remembered that the kinds of learning are limited as much by the biology of the species as by local conditions and opportunity. Human hunting, for example, could not be carried on in the small range characteristic of all the nonhuman primates, but human gathering also covers wide areas and man may adjust to seasonal changes in a way found in no other primate. The significance of range can best be understood if relevant characteristics of the central nervous system are also taken into account.'[15]

To live in a group and learn correct behaviour requires social discipline. The young must not stray into danger. They learn the skills necessary for survival through play but they must not annoy the elders. The troop must follow a recognized leader in search of food, there must be some drill to avoid or defy enemies, and the group must act together to defend their territory against rival groups. The mechanism which supplies the need for discipline is the establishment of a hierarchy of ranks. Rank is first of all determined by general categories: usually age (until senility) is superior to youth; in some species females are superior, and in many inferior, to males. Within these general classes individuals are ranked. This system has been observed amongst birds, and the expression 'pecking order' has passed into the language. It has been found that amongst jackdaws pecking order is established amongst

[15] ibid. p. 616-7.

males and that a mate takes her place in the hierarchy by marriage.[16]

The usual means of establishing dominance of one individual over others is the same as that used for the defence of territory. Thus amongst lemurs, who mark out their territory by means of scent, one will challenge another to a stink fight, and the winner establishes dominance when the loser admits defeat. Lorenz has pointed out the importance of a ritual for surrender and a mechanism in the victor that inhibits further attack when the signal of surrender is given. (Doves, who do not normally fight, lack this mechanism, so that when, through the accident of being caged together, they get into a fight, they fight to the death.)[17]

The fact that the response of recognizing the dominance of a superior is as much innate as the impulse to seek dominance over an inferior is established by a curious story. By accident, a lemur of one species was accepted into a troop of another species. He did not have their particular kind of stink glands or the capacity to recognize their stink. Thus he never knew when he was beaten and rose to a high position of dominance amongst them.[18]

It used to be supposed that the main point of the hierarchical system was in reproduction – the grand old man got the most wives. This may be the case amongst cocks and stags, but apparently not amongst the apes. Male chimpanzees, who in other respects are highly status conscious, have been seen to queue up amicably for a female on heat without regard to rank.[19]

Family and social relationships – a mother's care, the age-mates' challenge – are necessary to nourish and develop the emotional apparatus of the individual, which in turn makes social life possible for him. (Deprived monkeys

[16] Lorenz, *King Soloman's Ring*, p. 147, et seq.
[17] Lorenz, *Aggression*, p. 207. and *King Soloman's Ring*, p. 183–5.
[18] Jolly, op. cit., p. 123 et. seq.
[19] Jane Goodall, in *Primate Behaviour*, p. 455.

have been found to grow up with psychological mal-
formations.)

Social life requires communication. The apes communi-
cate by gestures, grimaces and sounds. Their vocalizations
for the most part convey moods and attitudes rather than
information.

'By far the greatest part of the whole system of communication seems to be devoted to the organization of social
behaviour of the group, to dominance and subordination,
the maintenance of peace and cohesion of the group,
reproduction, and care for the young. Inter-individual
relationships are complex enough in monkeys and apes to
require a communication system of this high order of
complexity. But there is little application of the communication system to events outside the group, beyond the
existence of signals signifying potential danger.'[20]

Moreover, the apes show none of the aptitude for
imitating sounds and learning to repeat them which is so
highly developed in song birds.[21] Their signals could not be
developed into a regular language that their children could
be taught.

At whatever point apes branched off from the main stem
of evolution, the requirements of social life produced
amongst them many characteristics which we recognize in
ourselves, implying sentiments of love, ambition, loyalty
and hostility to outsiders. Social life requires the transmission of lore and skill by learning; it gives rise to the
basic moral problem – a conflict of interest between the
individual and the group – which is solved by the capacity
to submit to an accepted code of behaviour. In any troop
there are marked differences of ability and temperament

[20] Peter Marler, in *Primate Behaviour*, p. 584.
[21] W. H. Thorpe and M. E. W. North, 'Origin and Significance
of the Power of Vocal Imitation', *Nature*, Vol. CCVIII, No. 5007,
October 16, 1965.

amongst individuals; there is a capacity for play and fun and an elementary pleasure in adornment. Man was once defined as a tool-making animal, but now it has been discovered that chimpanzees construct tools designed for particular uses.[22] The distinctive characteristic of mankind is the invention of language that conveys information about things not present and permits speculation about things not known. The apes have manners, it is language that makyth man.

---

[22] Reynolds in *Primate Behaviour*, p. 380, and Jane Goodall, ibid., p. 440.

2

ISOLATED ECONOMIES

WHEN man woke up, so to say, to conceptual thought, he presumably already had a level of social organization at least equal to that of the chimpanzees. He knew what to eat and where to find his food. He was accustomed to accepting certain rules of conduct and he recognized family relationships.

Just as the marsupials who have survived in Australia and the lemurs in Madagascar throw some light on the stage of physical evolution they had reached when they branched off from the main stem, so some human communities which have escaped from the march of history throw light upon the social development of primitive man. These societies are not themselves primitive.

The marsupials alive today had evolved very far along their own branch where they were free from placental competitors. The lemurs have a highly developed and differentiated pattern of social life, though they branched off before intelligence had got very far. Similarly, the communities that have been studied by anthropologists have languages and customs which are highly elaborated – a long way from the chimpanzees.

Each has developed in its own way. Those which are in contact with each other (friendly or hostile) recognize each other as people who are 'not like us', who have different speech and different ideas of proper behaviour. The accidents of geography kept them more or less completely isolated from the influence of the great literate civilizations, to provide our own self-conscious age with examples of the rich variety of solutions that have been found for the problems of human existance. (A kind of borderline case between isolation and connection is provided by societies, such as some Islamic tribes in Africa, who nominally adopted one or other of the great world religions without allowing it to have much effect upon their traditional way of life.)

Probably the mode of evolution of language can never be discovered, however many anthropoid skulls are dug up. The observation that apes lack the capacity (with which birds, and perhaps dolphins, are endowed) to imitate new sounds suggests that there was a great leap along the path of evolution after the side-road that led to the apes had left the main line. Language and the social and technical innovations which it made possible obviously had survival value. There is no reason to doubt that language evolved under the pressure of natural selection like other capacities, such as the problem-solving intelligence of the monkeys which defeated the lemurs. But once conceptual thought had been arrived at, it proved to have enormous possibilities that were, so to say, surplus to the requirements of physical existence. The interplay of consciousness with environment, of freedom with necessity, which is the characteristic of human life, was the consequence of the acquisition of language, over and above its technical advantage for survival.

This is seen in the rich elaboration in the forms of language and the uses to which it has been put by the peoples of which we know something (and they are a tiny fraction of all that have existed). They are found to have an imaginative view of life; they account for their own origins and the natural phenomena surrounding them in poetic legends and they have invented a great variety of gods and ghosts. No doubt it is important for the cohesion of a society to have its own myths, but the particular content of the myth was not bound by necessity; it was free to take whatever form imagination chose to build or inner needs suggested. Similarly in many species of birds the males display brilliant plumage of a particular pattern to which alone the females will respond; it does not matter what the colours are, so long as they are the colours of that species and no other. Psychologists observe a number of common themes in mythology which appear to correspond to elements in the emotional life of the individual.[1] Here, in another way, resemblances can be accounted for better by the coincidence of circumstances than by transmission through a common inheritance of traditions.

The isolated communities which survived to be studied by anthropologists would not have survived unless their way of life was adjusted to their environment but the stories that they told about themselves were not much concerned with economic affairs. Non-economic activity is not unknown amongst animals. The pelicans, whose economic life is all at water level, spend time soaring high in the air in the company of cranes. The elaboration of the dominance system amongst many species seems to be greater than is necessary for social discipline – it gives the creatures, so to say, an object in life beyond merely keeping alive.

In the isolated communities, it seems, economic activity was not thought of as aiming at economic ends. Customary methods of production provided for customary needs; needs were only indirectly for subsistence; directly they were governed by a system of religious and family obligations, elaborated in a great variety of ways. In all these communities (and, indeed, in the historic civilization) there was a strong emphasis upon kinship, incest taboos and family relationships. Mating, parenthood and sibship are the same for all mankind; with the capacity for reflection that language gave him, man built up numerous patterns of connections by birth and by marriage; economic life was woven into each pattern in a system of claims and duties. Moreover, offerings had to be made to priests, elders or chiefs. Even when such gifts were expected to be redistributed to the people, some usually stayed with the recipients, but this was not grudged, for in honouring the

---

[1] Cf. Anthony Storr, *Human Aggression*, p. 48.

chiefs or the gods the people were satisfying their own sense of honour.[2]

It is impossible precisely to define a surplus of production over the necessities of subsistence, because it is impossible precisely to define subsistence. Needs, as we know only too well, grow with the means to satisfy them. All the same, in any society there is some notion of a distinction between daily bread and something extra – for a guest, for a feast or for tribute to whom tribute is due. The imperative requirement to produce a surplus is useful for mere survival. It provides a margin that can be forgone in times of dearth. Enough is too little. Just as the incentive of hunger is needed to make us eat, so the incentive of good name and proper behaviour is necessary to keep an economy going.

In so-called civilized societies, it is the poor who spend their days in an anxious search for the means to live and the rich who can indulge in gratuitous activities; but when we compare rich and poor societies, the reverse often appears. The isolated communities, when they were discovered and brought into the frame of reference of 'national income per head', were placed very low on the scale, yet for many of them the proportion of energy, skill and mental activity devoted to non-economic aims was much greater than it is with us.

This was found to have been developed to a high pitch in the islands of the South Seas, where not much work is needed to grow yams and gather coconuts. There several communities developed various highly elaborate systems of social scoring around objects of no direct usefulness. The most famous of these was the Kula observed by Malinowski.[3] A number of archipelagos (including the Trobriand Islands) lie in a rough circle; the peoples inhabiting them took advantage of this to develop a system of partnerships passing gifts across each island and overseas. A set of

[2] George Dalton, in *Tribal and Peasant Economies*, (Edited by himself), p. 73.
[3] Malinowski, *Argonauts of the Western Pacific*.

necklaces of red beads were sent round clockwise and a set of white bracelets were sent round anti-clockwise. The relations between partners was not direct swapping. Each gave without return, but expected an equivalent gift in due course. Round the circle went the gifts, so that a particular piece re-appeared in each island once in about ten years. On the giving, rather than the receiving, was built up honour and prestige for individuals and for their tribe.

The notion of honour in giving, and the receiving of a gift implying acceptance of an obligation, plays a great part in many societies. The exchanges of armour and treasure between the Homeric heroes was on this pattern.[4] (There are vestigial remnants of it amongst ourselves, for instance in the custom of reciprocating invitations to dinner or standing rounds of drinks.)

Though the Kula exchanges had no economic purpose, they had important economic consequences. The islanders had to invest in canoes and to build up stocks of food to victual the voyages and to entertain visiting partners. (The voyages were often of hundreds of miles, requiring adventure and seamanship which caused Malinowski to call the islanders Argonauts.) Each tribe had a motive for acquiring a surplus and an acceptable manner of consuming it. Moreover, economic trade took place under the wing of the ritual exchanges. The voyagers carried goods not available in the island to be visited and bartered them for goods needed at home.

There are many examples amongst the peoples of Oceania of economic life thus organized around non-economic purposes. Amongst the peoples of Malekula in New Guinea there was a cult of pigs' tusks.[5] The upper tooth which would normally grind against the tusk is removed; the tusk grows into a spiral. Certain payments, such as bride price and compensation for adultery, could be made only in terms of tusked pigs; loans could be taken and were

[4] See M. I. Finley, *The World of Odysseus*, Chapter III.
[5] See John Layard, *Stone Men of Malekula*.

repaid with interest in the form of an increment in growth of the tusk. The cult of tusks gave an incentive to economic activity, for the pigs had to be fed and ritual feasts provided. Thus the community produced a surplus over its immediate needs and consumed it in the pursuit of honour amongst men and gods.

In Rossel Island[6] there was a system which appears to us even more gratuitously elaborate, though no doubt to its practitioners it seemed natural and obvious. There was a stock of two kinds of shell coins each with a hierarchy of ranks which determined the exchange values of the individual pieces, but these values applied only to particular transactions. A certain kind of coin had to be given at marriage, another type to the relatives of a man slaughtered for a cannibal feast, and so forth. There was a system of loans at interest, but each specific type of coin had its specific requirement of repayment, so that no exchange value of one type of coin with another was established. Certain useful or ritual objects could be exchanged with some coins of low rank, but for the most part the game consisted of acquiring prestige rather than physical wealth.

The concept of climbing a status pyramid by acquiring wealth, inheritance of wealth and status, the concept of interest connected with the value and the duration of a loan, the emergence of a profession of financiers to negotiate between lenders and borrowers, appear to the modern observer to resemble features of our own economic life, but both the institutions and the motivations of the islanders were very different from ours. The employment of the labour of others for profit was unknown; investment in means of production, such as canoes and fishing tackle, was limited to what a man's own family could use, or what a co-operating group could use co-operatively.

The game would have been spoiled if there were a one-

[6] See Loccaine Baric in *Capital, Saving and Credit in Peasant Societies*, (ed. Raymond Firth and B. S. Yamey), and George Dalton in *Tribal and Peasant Economies*.

way process of accummulation, so that a few families came
to own all the ceremonial wealth. The ritual of exchanges,
such as payments at marriage and at mortuary feasts or
the custom of distributing a man's accumulation at his
death in order to secure his spirit a satisfactory after-life,
helped to keep them circulating.

In Rossel Island the accumulation of economic wealth
(as opposed to the status-giving coins) was held in check
by the custom of one man challenging another to give a
feast. A competition then ensued to see who could dissipate
the most wealth.

A highly developed system which was devoted to
continuous and energetic accumulation without stultifying
itself by a progressive concentration of wealth grew up
amongst the Indians of North-west Canada.[7] A man could
acquire a place in a fixed hierarchy of honourable titles by
birth, by marriage, or by wiping out the former holder in
battle. To validate the succession to a title required a
potlatch ceremony – a lavish feast with a greatest possible
distribution of wealth to the assembled tribes. Each potlatch
was a challenge to the guests that had to be met by a
greater distribution in turn. The culminating feat in the
contest was the destruction of valuables. Certain copper
discs embodied the acme of prestige (like the highest
ranking coins in Rossel Island); one chief could defeat
another by throwing the most esteemed disc into the fire.
To back up their own chief and save him from shame,
each tribe was engaged in accumulating stocks; and minor
potlatches were carried out by commoners to celebrate events
in their own families; thus great energy was called forth
and productive activity kept at stretch. Contact with fur-
traders brought easy riches to the tribes and factory-made
blankets became the chief currency in the potlatch. At the
same time war was discouraged as an alternative means of
establishing social prestige. The potlatch system hyper-

[7] See Helen Codere, *Fighting With Property*. Monographs of
the American Ethnological Society, Number 18.

trophied and the distribution and destruction of wealth became more and more extravagant.

The Canadian administration outlawed the potlatch in the name of proper economic principles, but it took a century to stamp out the practice and reduce the proud tribesmen to getting a mere living in the lower ranks of civilized society.

The foregoing provide examples of how economic rationality for a community can be preserved as a by-product of beliefs and emotions in the individual which have no economic meaning at all. There are also examples of isolated communities in which the attitude to economic affairs was much more direct.

The following account, for instance, is given of the Bushong, a tribe in Central Africa.

'For the Bushong, work is the means to wealth, and wealth the means to status. They strongly emphasize the value of individual effort and achievement, and they are also prepared to collaborate in numbers over a sustained period when this is necessary to raise output.

'The Bushong talk constantly and dream about wealth, while proverbs about it being the stepping-stone to high status are often on their lips. Riches, prestige, and influence at court are explicitly associated together.'[8]

Wealth here has the straightforward meaning of food crops and household goods, though presumably the main benefit from it was its power to command respect from kinsmen and clients.

These people were observed after they had acquired some knowledge of the market economy, through the Government of the Belgian Congo. The reaction of various peoples to contact with the capitalist world is very various. Those who took easily to commercial life were, perhaps,

[8] Mary Douglas, in *Markets in Africa*, ed. G. Dalton, pp. 200-1.

those who had some corresponding element in their own institutions.

It is remarkable that close neighbours of the Bushong, the Lele, who appear to be related to them, have totally opposite notions of dignity and prestige which allows no scope for acquisitiveness.[9]

From the the rich variety of culture that remained to be studied in modern times, we can guess that the combination of articulate traditions with a capacity to learn from the experiments of original individuals gave mankind great freedom to construct institutions that were not closely bound by physical necessity. Yet at the same time, the habits of each community were contrived to fit the requirement of its habitat.

The isolated communities of the Pacific supported life mainly by cultivating vegetables; they must have brought their pigs with them. Australia was peopled at an earlier stage of development when man, like the apes, lived on what he could gather and catch from the surrounding plants, insects and animals. The Central Arctic provides no vegetables. There man developed a way of life dependent entirely upon hunting.[10] This was not primitive in the sense of being close to the apes. Presumably the ancestors of the Eskimo came from Asia accustomed to a mixed diet and were caught by the ice age in a region where survival required them to adopt appropriate customs. Similarly the handful of Bushmen who have survived in the Kalahari had to adopt a hard and meagre desert life, though their ancestors shared the abundant game of Africa with the lions.

The system of territory, for man as for other creatures, was an economic necessity; the area required to support a group depended on what it provided – in arid Australia a man, like a kangaroo, must 'walkabout' to get a living.

[9] Ibid.
[10] R. B. Lee, in *Man the Hunter*, ed. R. B. Lee and I. De Vore, p. 42.

Where food is plentiful, close settlement becomes possible. Sometimes the same area could provide overlapping territories for distinct communities who establish a symbiosis on the basis of different methods of exploiting its resources.[11]

The territorial animals defend their living-space by a variety of methods embodied in the biological inheritance of each particular species. Mankind, freed by language from set patterns of behaviour, comes up with the conception of property, or rightful ownership. Among the natives of the arid regions of Australia, for instance, where economic life was quasi-nomadic, each clan had its beloved homeland. The individual member of the group considered it to be his birthplace, even if his mother had happened to be travelling outside at the time when he was born. The range over which food could be gathered, however, was not exclusive; generosity and hospitality to other clans was considered a virtue.[12] Some tribes discouraged entry to their lands by wiping out parties of intruders when they were discovered;[13] but they recognized buffer zones between their claims and those of their neighbours.[14] Another peaceful method of securing frontiers (of which examples are found in India) was for each tribe to exchange womenfolk with its neighbours so that a whole area was covered by a network of kinsfolk respecting each other's territorial claims.[15]

A human society inhabiting an area where some necessity, such as salt, was unobtainable, required some kind of international exchange in order to survive, but they may have explained it to themselves in quite other terms, or, as in the Kula, necessary trade may have been incidental to ritual duties. Moreover, trade was not confined to necessaries.

[11] See John Turnbull, *Wayward Servants.*
[12] See L. R. Hiatt, in *Man the Hunter.*
[13] op. cit., Discussion, p. 158.
[14] ibid., p. 157.
[15] See B. J. Williams, in *Man the Hunter.*

The inhabitants of Norfolk in neolithic times had an export trade in flint axes and it seems that the main benefit they derived from it was the import of amber from the Baltic.[16] Presumably local resources provided necessities; bulk trade would not be possible over such distances; the beautiful exotic material was perhaps given a ritual significance or became the basis of social status.

How the exchanges took place we shall never know. They may have arisen from some system of gifts such as developed in the Pacific, or expressed a religious cult. It seems, however, that something like trade, as we know it, came into operation, for the axes developed into currency.[17] It is a fallacy of the economic text-books that barter requires a double coincidence – that I have an axe to spare and want amber just when you are in the converse position. Any durable object that is generally desired is *pro tanto* a vehicle for purchasing power. With your amber you could acquire more axes than you needed for your own use, and with them purchase whatever other goods you wanted, or hold them as a store of value to make purchases later or to acquire the prestige of an owner of wealth. One of the first uses of copper was to make symbolic axes that developed into a regular currency with coins of different denominations.[18]

Another kind of international relationship which evidently developed very early was warfare. Language and tradition are cohesive within a group but distinctive between groups. Humans are all of one species and (unluckily for some of them) can breed together. Groups separated for millenia acquired stocks of genes which produced characteristics suited to their conditions of life – darker skins and a greater capacity to sweat may have been an adaptation to living in hot climates – as well as many features which do not seem to have any particular use. These broad groups were split up into innumerable fragments differentiated by speech

[16] See J. G. D. Clark, *Prehistoric Europe*, p. 264.
[17] ibid., p. 250.   [18] ibid., p. 264.

and mythology, and amongst some of these weapons, presumably first developed for catching food or for defence against predators, began to be used for fighting.

Amongst the peoples who survived to be studied by anthropologists, two distinct types of warfare have been observed. The first is war as a kind of sport. Amongst the head-hunters of Borneo a young man had to prove himself by going out on an expedition to take a head from a neighbouring tribe, which ritual required when a chief died at home. In Malekula, an island would be divided into two sides between which disputes might be settled by fighting; and between the peoples of the small islands and of coastal regions of the large one, fighting also took place. The rule governing these wars was that there must be an equal number of dead on each side (usually two or three). Thus it was the victors who were in peril after each round and when the war (which involved ravaging the adversaries' gardens) became a nuisance, the winners would voluntarily give up a man of their own to be sacrificed and eaten so as to even the score and make peace possible.[19] The system was upset when one side acquired muskets from white traders and almost wiped out the other. This was a grave error which the victors bitterly repented when they found how it had spoilt their whole way of life.[20]

A stone-age people were discovered in a mountain valley in New Guinea who had remained isolated until 1961.[21] For them war between adjacent tribes was continuous, consisting of set battles and surreptitious raids. After each enemy death there was a ceremonial triumph at home, and after every death at home an elaborate funeral and plans for revenge. Killing was the basis of status. There was a category of 'worthless' men who feared or disliked fighting. They were not obliged to go to war but they were despised and could be robbed with impunity. War had no economic

[19] Layard, op. cit., p. 599.
[20] ibid., p. 603.
[21] See Peter Mathiesson, *Under the Mountain Wall.*

motive; land gave ample room for all; the population was
kept in check by the women resorting to abortion.[22] The
spoils of war were captured weapons, contributing to glory
rather than to wealth.[23] Murder and manslaughter within
the tribe were deprecated.[24]

Amongst other animals the fights over territory and the
struggle for status rarely result in death, and then only by
accident. A mechanism for surrender inhibits the victor.[25]
The emotional apparatus that permits men to enjoy killing
no doubt has its roots in the capacity for rage with which
other animals defend territory, but it has grown much
further. Students of morbid psychology connect the capacity
for hatred with the frustration due to a long helpless
childhood.[26] Whatever its emotional roots, it seems that
language and rationality gave rise to the concept of an
enemy. It may well be that war was responsible for hatred
and sadism, rather than hatred being responsible for war.

The qualities developed in war as sport were turned to
serious aims in the other type of warfare – conquest. One
people, who by superior technology or superior discipline
and organization could overcome others, drove the weak
from their lands, enslaved them or exacted tribute from
them. In several regions of Africa and China a small image
of racial domination survived independently of the great
imperialistic civilizations.

The first kind of warfare, like trade in ritual objects or
potlatch demonstrations, enables individuals within a society
to compete for prestige. It requires the production of a
surplus and provides a means of consuming it. (The Eskimos
could not indulge in it because their life was too hard.)
The second kind of warfare is the means by which one
group can extract a surplus from another. Both elements
are present in our own history.

Of all the multifarious types of social organization that

---

[22] op. cit., p. 27.
[23] ibid., p. 86.
[24] ibid, p. 31 and p. 76.
[25] Cf. above, p. 19.
[26] Storr, op. cit., p. 44.

mankind developed, very few have survived to be submitted to modern curiosity. Those which have, present great variety but many resemblances. The men who made them all had much the same emotional apparatus and capacity for developing intelligence through language. All were faced with the same set of problems – to secure an economic base, to regulate family life, and to establish the rules of proper behaviour and pass them on from generation to generation. These three sets of problems – economic, pro-creative, and political – man shares with the apes. A fourth was introduced by him – the organization of warfare.

For each problem a variety of solutions were possible (perhaps many were tried that did not prove viable); any solution that was found was embroidered with imaginative rationalizations which taught its followers that their solution was the right one. The resemblances that are found between various societies can sometimes be traced to inheritance of a common tradition but most appear to arise, like the resemblance between the profile of a dolphin and a fish, from the requirements of the situations in which they grew up.

3

LAND AND LABOUR

THE first form of agriculture may have been discovered by accident. Perhaps, when a forest fire had destroyed vegetation and driven off the game, people found that seeds would grow in the ash; in any case, it became a regular system to clear a certain area of forest by burning. Two crops can be taken from the same soil, and then it is necessary to move over to another patch. With sufficient territory a people could support themselves, the women planting and the men hunting, with very little work. In modern jargon, output per acre was very low, output per man-hour very high.[1] Total income, as in the South Sea Islands, could be whatever was necessary to provide the customary standard of consumption, with a surplus (if not for war) to support a chief, a priesthood, and to honour the gods. (People who live by this means today are accounted amongst the poorest; this is by contrast with the level of consumption that others obtain by working much harder.)

To restore the full cultivable capacity of a patch of forest requires about twenty years of fallow. The secondary growth is easier to clear than the virgin forest; the greatest return per unit of labour was secured when the territory was sufficient to allow one fifth to be cultivated at a time and when the whole area had been worked over at least once.

The skill and ingenuity of man upset the 'balance of nature'. He was able to feed and raise children at more than replacement rate so that the density of population within a territory gradually rose. At first, expansion of numbers could be accommodated by bringing new areas

[1] This and the following argument is derived from Ester Boserup, *Conditions of Agricultural Growth*.

of virgin forest into the cycle of cultivation, but when no more was available, the re-use of each patch began to speed up and the fallow to shorten, so that burning became too frequent to permit the regrowth of trees. The forest was destroyed and turned to bush or grassland.

Whether for this reason or because of a change of climate, men had to learn another way of getting a living. A similar line of development, about which much less is known, presumably went from preying upon flocks of beasts, such as the buffalo or the reindeer, to taming and breeding them.

Where water was available, agriculture and animal husbandry were united by the plough and settled cultivation became the basis of life.

Now the concept of property in land came into consciousness. Even in the system of shifting cultivation, it was convenient for each family to have its own garden within the burned patch, but each could have as much as they had labour and seed to cultivate; the area to be burned could be chosen to accommodate everyone. There was no cause for conflict and the legal system – that each family had a right to the crop that they had grown – no doubt seemed too obvious to need remark. This economic base could accommodate a great variety of systems of kinship and networks of mutual obligations such as have been observed among the isolated societies. With the plough, the legal system had to be adjusted to new technical conditions. Some tribes in Africa maintain to this day a system of common ownership. The land theoretically belongs to the chief, who distributes it to be worked in proportion to the labour available. Family inheritance, however, was a fairly obvious notion, and it proved to be a technical advantage since it brought the strong motive of family feeling into play as a stimulus to work and save. Matrilineal inheritance was the most straightforward system (it is a wise man who knows his own father) but where it still exists, a man finds it annoying to have to contribute to the income of his

sister's children, not his own. When animal husbandry took
over from hunting and the plough took over from the
digging stick, the economic position of men became
dominant and patrilineal inheritance came into fashion.

In medieval Europe, a system was developed of a fallow
of one year in three; animals grazing the fallow land
manured it. This system involved a whole village working
on a common plan; each family had some land in each
area so that they could claim a crop each year.

Under Hebrew law land was worked individually, but
a 'sabbath' had to be observed by all, providing a fallow
of one year in seven; this must have entailed the accumulation of stocks out of the produce of six working years.

The great density of population in some regions of Asia
made annual cropping necessary; provided irrigation and
fertilizers are available, rice can be grown continuously
on the same field. The animals have to be fed by cultivated
crops. (The man-hours required to provide for the beasts
have to be counted against the crops for human consumption.) In some parts of China the intensity of cultivation
was so great that even animals were not used; the plough
gave way to the hoe, human waste and river mud were
used for fertilizers and in some regions double or triple
cropping came into operation.

In India the great explosion of population set in only
recently; a pair of bullocks is still considered the indispensable minimum of equipment.

In Asian conditions individual cultivation was the rule,
though mutual aid in rush seasons was customary in some
neighbourhoods. Tradition and prudent attachment to
known methods imposed almost as much uniformity as the
common programme required by the three-field system.

In some regions of pre-Columbian America a dense
population was supported by the hoe; draft animals and
the wheel were unknown.

Given geography and climate, an increase in population
in any region required an increase in output per acre at

the expense of a decrease in output per man-hour of work. (A population which could not adapt its technique as density grew would either be wiped out or would migrate to conquer other lands.) The changes which increased density requires may bring a revolution in the whole basis of society as well as in technique, like the adoption of the plough, or they may take place by a gradual continuous pressure, like the fragmentation of holdings that end by animal power giving place to more and more intensive human labour.

Throughout recorded history, peasants have been the prey of civilization, and in recent time there are few remaining who have not been drawn into either the market or the socialist economic system, but it is possible to reconstruct from remnants here and there how a free society of cultivators would have evolved.

We may suppose that, when holdings were adequate with the known technique, labour was the limiting factor. Each family did no more work than was needed to supply its own requirements, and obligations including contributions to accepted public expenses for administration and religion.

In such an economy almost the whole of a family's production was for its own consumption. Accumulation might consist in breaking in new land, increasing livestock, building, and making tools. In respect to livestock, accumulation entails refraining from consumption – to rear a calf instead of slaughtering it – but other kinds of investment would entail extra work rather than forgoing consumption; indeed, they might entail extra consumption, for harder work requires more calories.

Even from neolithic times there were evidently specialists; mining and making flint tools and weapons required knowledge and skill as well as access to special natural resources. (Whether particular individuals were whole-time specialists or not must have depended upon the size of the community. In a small group, the specialists would spend part of their time as ordinary cultivators.) Specialization entails exchange. Adam Smith argued that, between equals, goods would exchange at the ratio of the amounts of labour needed to produce them but an equal amount of labour had no meaning where, by the nature of the case, each sort of labour was different. From the earliest times various kinds of services were, no doubt, valued at different rates – the priest was more honoured than the barber – and the payment in terms of grain for the skill of the blacksmith or the thatcher had to be set at a level that would allow them what the community considered a suitable standard of life. Since yields varied from year to year with the weather, such payments might be in terms of a share of the harvest rather than a specific quantity of grain. The lore of the specialist and his tools would be handed down from father to son on the same system as property in land. Various types of inheritance are possible – succession of the eldest son on the death of his father (or on his retirement to seek salvation, a practice common in Buddhist societies and not unknown elsewhere), joint inheritance of sons, a division of property amongst sons, or amongst all children. Marriage may require a payment to the bride's family or a dowry from her family. Patriarchial societies commonly have the concept of bastardy or superior and inferior wives. Bastards and younger sons excluded from inheritance, unless some other way of life was open, would have to serve their relations and be fed by them. In sophisticated societies it seems it was the anxiety of a man to know that his heirs were his own that lead to the cult of female virginity and the concept of the 'honour' of a daughter, sister or wife, 'The chastity of women,' as Dr Johnson said, 'is of the utmost importance, as all property depends on it.'[2] It may also have had other roots in the magical notions of primitive peoples. In some societies it became the basis of a kind of sport such as is depicted in the Restoration comedies – to seduce the

[2] James Boswell, *Life of Dr. Johnson* (Allen and Unwin edition) Vol. II, p. 86.

females of other men and protect one's own. In most
societies it was accompanied by the institution of prostitu-
tion to reconcile excess male sexuality with the requirements
of the family system.

The problems of the family are connected not only with
the economic basis of life but also with social organization.
Property in land and livestock provide a vehicle for competition in status – to this day we talk of a *big* man as one who
has large possessions. Through property, family relationships were drawn into the struggle. Where bride-price was
the custom, daughters were a valuable asset; where dowries
were required they were a drain upon the family's resources.
It was an advantage to a man to have many sons to work
his land, but a drawback to have many brothers to share it
with him.

Under whatever systems of inheritance, the chances of
family life would bring about changes in the relation of
property in land to labour available to work it, so that some
families would find themselves with more land than they
could cultivate and some with less. Moreover, differences
of temperament come in. Some men are industrious and
acquisitive, others feckless, idle or generous. There is a
certain tendency to check accumulation. The richer family
marries its children earlier, so that numbers increase faster
and land per head is reduced in the third generation. But
this tendency has generally proved too weak to offset the
forces pressing against equality.

In a society which allows inequality of possessions
between families, it perpetuates itself. Those with excess
land can make use of the labour of others, either by employing them at wages or letting land to them for a share of
the produce. Either way, property becomes a source of
income independently of its owner's work.

Where crops are seasonal, another source of property
income presents itself. Even where there is land available
to be broken in to cultivation, to take advantage of it a man
needs supplies of seed, tools, perhaps draft animals, and

certainly subsistence over the period from seed time to harvest. Those who have not enough to live upon till the next harvest can maintain themselves by taking a loan, promising repayment when the harvest comes in. From this the conception of interest – repayment by more than what was received, naturally arises. Thus a family which enjoys a surplus over its needs can increase its income still further by lending at interest. The maximum interest that can be extracted is the difference between what a man can produce in a year's work on the land available and what he must consume to live. Within that limit, the rate may be settled by custom at some round figure. Among the Hausa, before they were drawn into the modern monetary economy, 'two bundles of guinea corn had to be repaid at harvest for every one lent in the early farming season or, if the lender was generous, three bundles for every two lent.'[3] Thus a man who had twice as much corn as he needed to consume could eat one portion and lend one. He would then receive the whole back at the next harvest, lend half again, and so continue indefinitely without doing any more work or saving, living upon 'unearned income'. The generous lender who charged 50 per cent instead of 100 per cent was presumably a landowner who did not care to take full advantage of the poverty of his neighbours. The prohibition of interest and the jubilee year at which all debts were cancelled in Hebrew law, were designed to check accumulation from this source. From the system of loans developed the system of pledging land as security. This enabled the wealthy families to acquire the holdings of defaulting debtors. Families which lost their land had to become wage earners or tenants. Since family life was bound up with property, a class of landowners could become established within which marriages took place, and a class of labourers

[3] Firth op. cit., p. 30. Professor Firth, reckoning in market terms, maintains that the value of repayment was cancelled out by the fall in price of corn after the harvest, but this is not relevant to the generation of property income in terms of corn.

who had only poverty to leave to their children. Romantic tales of the tragic conflict between love and duty were told in many languages.

An independent family owning sufficient land to support themselves could work as much as they felt to be worthwhile. (This freedom was limited where cultivation had to be in common, as in the three-field system, but even there some could take more trouble than others.) By putting in more work over a year the family would gain a greater product, either by cultivating a larger area of their holding or by more intensive work, for instance on weeding. They would aim to produce as much as they required to live without exerting themselves excessively. In economists' jargon, they would balance the utility of income against the disutility of work. A family which owned no land would have to work much harder. A share-cropper who has to give half the gross produce of a plot of land in order to be allowed to work on it must produce more than twice as much as a free family controlling the same area if he is to eat as well as they. (More than twice, for he is giving away half the gross produce and must find the seed from his own half.) To gain twice the produce, he must work more than twice as hard. In economists' jargon, after a certain point there are diminishing returns to labour applied to a given area within a given agricultural technique, so that, say, an extra 10 per cent of man hours worked over a year yields less than 10 per cent extra produce. Depending on the nature of the soil and the technique in use, it may be impossible for him to produce enough to support the same standard of life as the independent family, so that he not only works harder but eats less.

The landowning family, on the other hand, can consume more than the free family and work less. The first use to which they put the surplus they are acquiring is usually to keep their womenfolk from working in the fields. Next they employ servants or domestic slaves so that their women need not work in the home either, and finally the sons also are excused from working. Agents and strong-arm men are employed to make sure that the tenants pay up, and the priest, sharing their ample fare, preaches resignation to the poor.

At any moment, the level of rents and interest are fixed by custom and the use of round numbers, but there is a crude element of supply and demand in the situation. When the population is increasing, the demand for land is growing. The landlord can get tenants for smaller plots, so that they must work harder to live. The total produce of a given area rises and the landlord's income with it. Even if land is available for new settlement, the poor can make no use of it with their bare hands. Landlords can settle new villages and advance them what they need until they begin to pay. In economists' jargon, increase in population reduces the marginal product of labour and raises the marginal product of land, so that average income falls while the wealth of the landowner rises.

Malthus startled the humanitarian eighteenth century with the doctrine that the growth of population everywhere exceeds the growth of food supplies, and will be held in check by misery and starvation. From the foregoing analysis of the consequences of family property in land it seems clear that the Malthusian misery would set in when (with the available technique) the maximum amount of labour that a man could put forth in a year was not able to yield enough to support life. But then he would have no surplus to hand over to the landlord or the money-lender. He is reduced to misery, long before that stage is reached, by their exactions.

But if there were no landlords there would be no surplus, for free families would have no motive to produce more than they needed to consume.

4

RACE AND CLASS

PROPERTY interlacing with family relationships might generate a class of landowners in peaceful conditions but its most frequent origin has been in warfare. We do not know whether war developed first as a sport or as a form of hunting – to prey upon men when other game was scarce; we do know that no part of the world (except perhaps the arctic circle) has been immune from it in one form or the other.

Where neighbours are at the same technical level, with weapons which are not too powerful, like the stone-age peoples observed in New Guinea,[1] warfare can go on indefinitely. As the technical level rises, with the use of metals, the class system which may be loosely called feudalism emerges. The gentlemen fight and organize fighting, while the cultivators are obliged to support them by providing an agricultural surplus over and above their own consumption and to allow their sons to be recruited to fill the ranks of the armies. The cultivators in each area have a compelling motive to support their own gentlemen, for if not the gentlemen of another area would raid and slaughter them.

When one group can overwhelm another, by larger numbers, superior organization, the emergence of a powerful leader or the development of a higher level of effectiveness in weaponry and tactics, then war becomes conquest.

Over many parts of the world, in times now lost to history, one people have driven another, less well equipped for war, out of their lands and settled themselves there. In recent times this has been seen when the Bantu took over Southern Africa from the Bushmen and when the Christians took over North America.

[1] See p. 33 above.

More often the conquered people remained to work and hand over their surplus to new masters. When the conquerers were already organized in a social hierarchy, lands with cultivators to work them were allotted to gentlemen and lower ranks were stepped up above the new lowest order consisting of the old inhabitants of the land.

Another economic use of warfare was the capture of slaves. The system of using slaves to cultivate the land while gentlemen are occupied with war was seen in a number of African kingdoms. Its most famous example (apart from modern times) was the Athenian empire. (Sparta depended less upon captured slaves than upon a native population whom they used as helots.) A society, however, cannot consist only of gentlemen and slaves. There must be a sufficiently large free population of lower ranks who identify themselves with the gentlemen and enable them to keep the slaves in order. In Athens the aristocracy were those families who owned enough land and slaves to support their sons as horse-riding knights, while infantry was provided by yeomen farmers who owned few slaves and worked themselves. The overseers and strongarm men required to manage the large estates were often slaves promoted by the gentlemen to keep their fellow slaves at work. The domestic slaves, like Uncle Tom, had less need of force to keep them in order. Continuous war was necessary to keep up the supplies of fresh captives.[2]

In another type of organization, a central government controlled both military and civil affairs; power and authority was embodied in the heir of a princely dynasty – a Pharaoh or an Inca – who claimed the right to tribute directly from the cultivators and redistributed the surplus to his administrative officials and military commanders.

A centre of military power can augment its income in two further ways. The first is to subdue the governments of neighbouring lands, and, leaving them in charge, to exact

[2] See M. I. Finley in *Slavery in Classical Antiquity*, edited by himself.

tribute from them, which they are obliged to extract from the surplus of their own people. The second is to set up colonies to dominate the natives in outlying regions, or to cultivate their lands (with slaves or with the colonists' own labour) and to require remittances to the homeland.

These four ways – feudalism, central administration, imperialism and colonization – in which the agricultural surplus can be extracted for the benefit of a dominant class, have been repeated, in various permutations and combinations, throughout history from neolithic times to the present day.

Whether the land was worked by slaves, serfs or peasants, and the surplus was taken by independent gentlemen or by officers of a monarch, or of an imperialist power, the main lines of economic relations were the same. The surplus was consumed partly in maintaining a military establishment and partly in supporting the standard of life of the gentlemanly class. The expenditure of their households led to a great increase of handicraft production. Arms, dress, furniture, carriages, as well as works of art dedicated to the gods, required specialized skill. The few and simple craftsmen in the free villages were supported by contributions from the cultivators; now craftsmen were clients of the wealthy and earned a share of their rents by serving their requirements for martial power, comfort and display.

When a hundred families are paying half their produce to one landlord, his family does not want to eat a hundred times as much grain as a cultivator's (besides, meat, fruit and honey may be supplied to his household as extra dues). Part of his share in the grain goes to support producers of agricultural raw materials (silk, cotton or wool) and miners or foresters, and the rest to supporting his clients. Those amongst them who are builders and manufacturers partly supply each other's needs. Thus the grain that the cultivator parts with becomes, through skill and art, transmogrified into great wealth and splendour.

Cities grew up around forts where people and cattle

could retire from attack, and around temples and palaces. Intermediate classes were established between the cultivators and the landowners, of craftsmen, traders, financiers and clerks to cater to the needs of the wealthy households and of priests and learned men who shared their benefits.

When peace was preserved for long spells, huge agglomerations of population formed great cities, provisioned by the surplus that cultivators, one way or another, were obliged to produce and part with.

The ratio of townsmen to cultivators depended upon the fertility of the land, the productivity of known methods of agriculture (in particular the control of water) and upon the level of consumption allowed to the cultivator.

Where the harvest is seasonal, armies of manpower could be organized (fed from the product of their own labour) in the slack of the year, both for building and for fighting. Among martial castes in India, the autumn festival celebrates the opening of the campaigning season. It was presumably by this means that the valleys of the Nile, the Indus, the rivers of Mesopotamia and the Mekong were furnished with the stupendous monuments whose few remnants amaze us today.

Besides conquest, there was a source of wealth in foreign trade. The accumulation of an agricultural surplus in the palace, the temple or landowner's households provided scope for a market in exotic luxuries. Exchanges of necessaries for mass consumption might occur between neighbouring tribes with different resources – say hunters with cultivators, but when travel was difficult and dangerous long-distance trade could be only in goods which had a high value in proportion to their bulk. (This is just as much true when exchanges were given a ritual or political meaning as when prices and profit entered in.) The cost in grain of an imported good consists in the grain required to support the labour to make the export for which it is exchanged and to support and defend the emissary who carries it. Temples, palaces and wealthy households could

be adorned with exotic products or manufactures from
exotic raw materials because they could, one way or another,
purchase them with grain.

Herodotus remarked that there were no markets in
Persian cities.[3] The process of supplying food and raw
materials to an urban community could be organized by
the collection of dues, storage and distribution as salaries,
fees and offerings carried out in the name of the head of
state. Similarly exchanges of goods and services within the
urban community, and the values at which they took place,
could be regulated by custom and ranks attached to various
occupations. The concept of trade for profit presumably
arose from exchanges between peoples who appeared to
each other as foreigners, outside the rules and obligations
of the domestic society. Long-distance trade carried out by
intermediaries was free at both ends. Phoenicians and Arabs
who specialized in sea transport were under no ritual
obligations at either end of the voyage. Aristotle deplored
the unnatural activity of making money, which had become
established in his day, compared to the natural activity of
meeting the needs of the household and the community.[4]

From merchant trade grew up an intermediate medium
of exchange. This made it possible to sell one set of goods
without having to buy another immediately. Moreover it
was convenient to express values in terms of some common
measure. Gold (first used in the Greek colony of Lydia)
proved to be an excellent material for the purpose. From
foreign trade, money invaded the home economy; many
exchanges of goods and services came to be made through
the medium of money payments. Money prices, money
salaries and money taxes took over from the system of payments in kind.

The concept of investment for the sake of profit also
grew out of foreign trade. The merchant needed finance

[3] See Karl Polanyi, in *Trade and Market in the Early Empires*,
(edited by himself and others), p. 16.
[4] ibid., p. 64, et seq.

to provide the expenses of shipping, camel train or porters as well as the goods whose sale would replace the finance with an adequate excess to reward him for the risk and trouble and enable him to venture again on a larger scale. Interest which had been frowned upon as usury when it arose from the necessities of the cultivator, now took on a different guise, and calculations more subtle than 100 per cent return on corn came into use. Whole cities flourished upon trade and a profession of financiers came into being. This also leaked back from foreign trade into domestic production, but down till the dawn of the modern age in Europe and till today in societies which European culture has not yet swallowed up, the intrusion of the profit motive into domestic production was held in check by regulations based on status and the concept of a just price which would give every man a standard of life appropriate to his position in society.

A hierarchical society required to justify itself. Most often the dominance of one group of families over the rest was rationalized in terms of 'race'. The notion of 'us' and 'the others', connected with rules about whom it is proper to marry, arose wherever peoples of different language and habits were in contact with each other. Each might have a feeling of superiority to the other. Now superiority became asymmetrical. Better fed, taught to cultivate strength and courage, or devoted to subtle scholarship, the beneficiaries of the system could feel themselves different beings from the slaves or peasants who supported them, and could expect to be acknowledged as such.

Marriage rules were tightened up to prevent their 'blood' from mingling with that of their inferiors. In most societies this rule applied to the women of the superior families – the men were free to get bastards and half-castes and occasionally to elevate a beauty to the rank of marriage. Some, such as the Hebrews in Palestine and the Brahmans in India, taught that it was as much a crime for a man as for a woman to mingle blood (though practice did not necessarily follow precept). The concept of 'race' was reinforced when there was some marked difference in the appearance of the superior and inferior peoples. The most common has been colour, but anything will serve. The Japanese despised the Hairy Ainu not for being white but for growing beards. Aristotle maintained that slaves were inferior beings, though many were descended from prisoners taken in wars between Greek cities of the same stock as their masters. The concept of class as something in the order of nature was carried through the feudal ages in Europe down to modern times. Shakespeare, who depicts Henry V as a democratic king, gives him these sentiments:

On, on you noblest English!
Whose blood is fet from fathers of war-proof;

*   *   *

Be copy now to men of grosser blood
And teach them how to war. And you, good yeomen,
Whose limbs were made in England, show us here
The mettle of your pasture; let us swear
That you are worth your breeding.

The concept of status by birth reached its highest development in the caste system in India, where it is associated with a 'racial' preference for the fair skin of the Asian invaders over the dark colour of the natives.

Birth might establish power but talent was also necessary, for a state requires a bureaucracy and a legal system. For this, writing is a great convenience, but it is not indispensable. In the highly elaborate organization of the Incas, intelligence was conveyed by knots in string. In the kingdom of Dahomey, which flourished in the eighteenth century on the export of slaves captured from neighbouring peoples, a census of every village and a record of its taxable capacity was kept annually by a system of counting pebbles.[5]

The one great empire which has a continuous recorded

[5] See Karl Polanyi, *Dahomey and the Slave Trade*, Chapter III.

history from the bronze age to the present century developed bureaucracy to its highest level. The challenge of a scholar to the first Han emperor : 'You conquered this country in a chariot – can you rule it from a chariot?' was repeated in every age of Chinese history. (The Mongol conquest was a brutal interruption of continuity, but Kubla Khan took over the Chinese system of administration, and so did the Manchu dynasty which saw the end of the story.)

For 1500 years the personnel of the administration – civil service, judiciary and court – was recruited by a system of written examinations. The subject of study was classical texts which were assumed to instil moral principles rather than any particular branch of technical knowledge. This system gave prestige to learning above military prowess; a great part of the surplus was dedicated to cultivating the arts of civilization.

In China class was not based upon conceptions of 'race'. The Han people regarded themselves as all of one race; landlords recognized peasants in their villages as their fellow clansmen; in theory everyone was free to become a mandarin. But to learn characters and study the classics required expensive tuition and years free from work. Coming from an illiterate home, even the most devoted could take only the first step in learning – it was said to take three generations to get through the national examination. Thus learning and soft hands not used to toil became the mark of superiority. In Heian Japan, at the court of Prince Genji's father, the arts were cultivated in imitation of China, and the delicate aristocracy regarded the peasants (even more than Henry his yeoman) as creatures of grosser blood.

In India the concept of 'race' was applied even to learning; to this day it is commonly believed that Brahmans are more intelligent than people of other castes.

In feudal Europe illiterate gentlemen depended upon the Church to provide them with educated personnel; the institution of a nominally celibate clergy made it possible to recruit talent from the lower ranks of society without interfering with the family structure of the feudal class.

All the great religions that mankind has invented deprecate the worship of wealth and power but all have compromised with it, church or temple supporting the secular authority or setting up as an authority on its own account.

The combination of religion with the concept of status by birth has many times produced the institution of the divine monarch who is both the titular head of the administration and the intermediary of his people with the gods. A head of state to give unity of command was necessary, particularly for governments imposed by conquest, and the notion of a monarch passing power to his eldest son arose naturally where patrilineal inheritance was established. There have been elected monarchs – the chiefs of some African tribes, the Polish kings, the successor to Hamlet and the Holy Roman Emperors – but even then the candidates were confined to those with 'royal blood'.

When family succession was the rule, there could be no guarantee of an adequately gifted heir appearing in each generation. A convenient solution was sometimes found by building up the ritual character of the monarch and keeping power out of his hands. In Japan, for instance, a single dynasty which traces its ancestry to the sun has reigned throughout recorded history, while for long periods (interrupted by feudal wars) one or other of the great families administered the country. A similar pattern on a small scale was evolved by the Ranas in Nepal, who taught the king to believe that he was a reincarnation of Vishnu.

In China each dynasty established the divinity of its line; but Chinese political philosophy contained the principle of 'the mandate of heaven', which gave the people a legitimate right to overthrow a dynasty whose government degenerated. Perhaps the failure of the western Roman empire to find a satisfactory principle of succession contributed to its decline and fall.

5
COMMERCE AND NATIONALITY

TRADE and manufactures provided a source of wealth not directly dependent upon property in land, though indirectly dependent upon the expenditure of the agricultural surplus. In centres here and there around the world from China to Peru, a bourgeoisie grew up – that is, a community of townsmen, drawing an income from commercial activities, and enjoying a less or greater degree of independence from the court and the feudal powers. The most successful amongst them employed workers – as handicraftsmen, porters, seamen, entertainers and servants, so that a hierarchy based upon money income was established, and a market where agricultural produce could be sold for cash.

In Western Europe the money economy gradually invaded feudal agriculture. In England, feudalism had been superimposed upon Saxon village communities practising cultivation in the open field system. Rent was extracted by the lord owning a demesne (and sometimes strips in the open fields) which had to be cultivated without payment. The cultivators were serfs attached to the land. But servile labour is inefficient and troublesome to manage. Landlords gradually found it more convenient to employ full-time workers on the best parts of the demesne (with the services of the villagers at the harvest) and let off the rest of their lands for rent, in the form of commutation of dues expressed in terms of labour.

Moreover a money economy grew up beside this system with the wool trade. Bourgeois communities of manufacturers in Italy and the Netherlands imported English wool. The lords kept large flocks and the cultivators could graze a few sheep on the common lands.

In the thirteenth century, it seems, a rise in population created a scarcity of land. Supply and demand favoured the landlords. By one means or another, the cultivators' share in production was squeezed down. Hungry, landless families were shaken out at the bottom of the social structure. (Merrie England began to show the sad features of modern India.)[1]

Relief came by dreadful means. On a long-term decline in the growth of numbers was superimposed the violent shock of the Black Death, which wiped out perhaps a third of the populations that it attacked.[2] In England feudal serfdom, already disintegrating, was shattered beyond recovery. Rebel peasants raised the immortal cry:

> When Adam delved and Eve span
> Who was then the gentleman?

In Western Europe generally, the depopulation speeded up the liberalizing influence of money within the framework of feudalism. But east of the Elb the landlords were able to recover their grip and riveted serfdom in the necks of the cultivators more firmly than before.[3]

In England, the wool trade played a great part in finally digesting feudalism into the commercial system. The Black Death reduced the cultivated area needed for subsistence, leaving room for pastures, and at the same time the loss of rents inclined the landowners to look for another way of making their property yield income. Moreover, the feudal style of consuming the surplus in fighting over the inheritance of titles was obsolescent. With the internal peace that the Tudor monarchy imposed upon the warring nobility, land began to be seen as a source of wealth calculated in money rather than of the command of a tenantry to arm and lead to battle.[4] Sheep were more

[1] See M. Postan, in *Cambridge Economic History*, Vol. I, p. 552 et seq.

[2] ibid., p. 609.

[3] See L. Genicet in *Cambridge Economic History*, Vol. I, p. 739.

[4] The following argument is derived from Barrington Moore, *Social Origins of Dictatorship and Democracy*.

valuable than men. Numbers gradually recovered, but the landlords were no longer so keen to get tenants.

'During the sixteenth century the most significant of the "enclosures" were "encroachments made by lords of manors or their farmers upon the land over which the manorial population had common rights or which lay in the open arable fields." Propelled by the prospect of profits to be made either in selling wool or by leasing their lands to those who did and thereby increasing their rents, the lords of the manor found a variety of legal and semi-legal methods to deprive the peasants of their rights of cultivation in the open fields and also their rights to use the common for pasture of their cattle, the collection of wood fuel, and the like.

*   *   *

'Clearly a substantial amount of land formerly subject to customary rules prescribing the methods of cultivation was becoming land to be used at the discretion of the individual. Simultaneously the commercialization of agriculture meant a change from the feudal seigneur who was at worst a lawless tyrant and at best a despotic parent to an overlord who was closer to an acute man of business exploiting the material resources of the estate with an eye to profit and efficiency.

*   *   *

'Those who promoted the wave of agrarian capitalism, the chief victors in the struggle against the old order, came from the yeomanry and even more from the landed upper classes. The main victims of progress were as usual the ordinary peasants.'[5]

[5] Barrington Moore, op. cit., p. 9–11. The quotation in the first paragraph is from Tawney, *The Agrarian Problem*, p. 150.

Thus commerce invaded the home economy. At the same time the growth of sea power, the first colonies in the New World and the great profits of the slave trade gave commercialism a powerful support from overseas.

The Civil War has been interpreted as an attack upon the last bastion of feudalism.[6] The very fact that it was turned against the Crown set England on the path to democratic capitalism. The Restoration could not reverse the tide. Commerce became associated with liberty.

The enclosures of the sixteenth century reduced rural labour. 'Sheep ate men.' In the eighteenth century, the tide turned; enclosures then were a means of introducing intensive labour techniques. A rise in population set in. (It is believed to have been due in the first instance to a fall in death rates, which, however, has not been satisfactorily explained.) Injected into a system where agriculture was already largely commercialized, it brought into use crop rotations and stall feeding of cattle to eliminate the triennial fallow and bring nearly all cultivable land into use every year.[7] To apply these techniques required enclosures. The great estates inherited from feudal times were let out in farms and the peasants became wage labourers, deprived of the last of their ancient rights.

> Tis bad enough in man or woman
> To steal a goose from off a common;
> But surely he's without excuse
> Who steals a common from the goose.[8]

The destruction of feudalism in France took another course which left agriculture in the hands of peasant proprietors.[9]

The development of towns and cities had made food an article of commerce as much in France as in England but

---

[6] op. cit., Chapter 1.
[7] See Boserup, op. cit., p. 38.
[8] See *Oxford Book of Quotations*, p. 527b.
[9] See Barrington Moore, op. cit., Chapter II.

while the enclosures were raising agricultural productivity
in England there was little change in France. 'Except for
the introduction of maize during the sixteenth century as
a forage crop for animals, which increased greatly the
amount of wheat that could be marketed, there were no
important technical innovations. Agriculture continued to
be carried on in fundamentally the same technical and
social framework as had existed during the Middle Ages . . .
the nobles used the prevailing social and political framework to squeeze more grain out of the peasants and sell it.'[10]

The peasants supported the Paris mob who were the
spearhead of the French Revolution in smashing the
aristocracy, destroying feudal privilege and breaking up the
estates of the nobility and the church into small freeholds.
Beyond that they had no use for radical ideas. Liberty,
Equality and Fraternity ended up as the charter for private
property.

In Central Europe the peasant revolts of the sixteenth
century were defeated and bloodily repressed.[11] In East
Germany feudalism was modernized but not relaxed;
serfdom was introduced into Russia. In the Peninsula,
feudalism freed the land from the Moors and went on to
create overseas empires. Its remnants survived to overthrow
the short-lived Spanish republic of 1935, and to maintain
the last African empires till today. In Sweden feudalism
never took root so that no upheaval was needed to install
democracy. In West Germany and Italy bourgeois societies
grew up around the courts of princelings or on the proceeds
of trade.

In this little continent, so many various ways were found
to transform the agricultural surplus into the basis of
national wealth and power and each left its mark upon
national history.

The sentiment of nationalism attached to a country
rather than a city or a neighbourhood had grown as
feudalism declined. War brought it into consciousness. The

[10] op. cit., p. 53.   [11] ibid., p. 466.

attempts of the English Crown to claim dominion in France, which began as feudal sport, ended by involving the populace on both sides in a sense of national identity.[12]

The very fact of having a government over a particular area creates a centre for patriotism to crystalize around. We see today national sentiment building up within the perfectly arbitrary rectangles which the European empires drew on the map of Africa. A government is bound to be concerned with the economic affairs of its subjects, if only to establish the basis for taxation. National power has always been used (even under the guise of laissez faire) to promote national interests. Yet the sentiment of patriotism is not directly self-regarding for the individual. In war it commands the greatest sacrifices and in economic affairs for the mass of a population it has often meant a preference for being exploited and commanded by people of the same language and colour as oneself, rather than any great hope of personal gain.

Perhaps the propensity to identify the ego with a group larger than the family has its roots in the same emotional apparatus which gives social cohesion to a company of apes, but the capacity to attach it to abstract conceptions is merely human. Mr Ardrey[13] explains the intense rage which he felt on hearing of the raid on Pearl Harbor as being due to an instinct for territory but it was not uninstructed instinct that made him, in a flat in New York, identify his territory with the island of Honolulu.

However that may be, it is clear enough that national patriotism was developed and systematized in Western Europe along with the commercialization of social relationships, and that it gave national governments great support in the schemes of economic expansion through conquest and trade which soon brought everyone under their sway and in the end, by revulsion, spread national feeling to the rest of the world.

[12] ibid., p. 418.
[13] *The Territorial Imperative*, p. 230.

6

CAPITALIST EXPANSION

FROM one point of view the whole of human history from the neolithic to the eighteenth century can be treated as one period and the Industrial Revolution till today as another. Many of the same patterns repeat themselves. The British Empire had something in common with the Roman; the destruction of Greece through internecine war leading to the dominance of Macedon are repeated in this century in European wars leading to the dominance of the United States. But there are three characteristics of the modern age which distinguish it from the past – the hypertrophy of the nation state (which some modern attempts at international-ism have done little to check), the application of science to production and the penetration of money values into every aspect of life.[1]

The change cannot be attributed to any single cause. It was as though a spark fell into a great heap of tinder that had been accumulating for centuries.

It required a great development of science – not so much in knowledge of the material world as in the scientific point of view. Science and mathematics were developed in Babylon and Egypt, less successfully in China, in order to work out from the study of the heavens a calender, for the correct observation of religious ceremonies and for use in agriculture. But for the most part the human race, even today, does not attach importance to the distinction between a thing being the case and not being the case. Myths, superstitions and slogans satisfy them. Logic, inquiry by experiment and a rationalist view of history were highly developed in Athens, but since they were the occupation of gentlemen, methods of production were not much affected by them. In Rome, Byzantium, and medieval Europe, the thread was lost. The Renaissance, and then

[1] Cf. E. J. Hobsbawm, *Industry and Empire*.

the Reformation, prepared the way for a revival of rationalism. Protestantism was an important pre-condition for the Industrial Revolution, not so much because of any particular doctrines that it proclaimed as because it was a break with orthodoxy and obscurantism.

There was a technical reason why the mathematics of the ancient world had little application to technology. Algebra and geometry were developed as speculative philosophy but the humble uses of arithmetic were impeded by the clumsy system of numerals. The Arabs learned from India where another system of speculation had introduced the notion of zero and positional notation. In the fourteenth century the Church fought hard against the introduction of this system into Europe[2] but its practical advantages were too great. Without it engineering would never have got far.

Another element in the heap of tinder that took fire in the Industrial Revolution was the introduction of printing from China and the spread of literacy among the laity.

Why was England in particular the scene? The development of industry required an increase in the agricultural surplus to support a growing urban population. The new methods of farming introduced in the eighteenth century provided it. Moreover the enclosures turned peasants into landless labourers. It was no longer possible for growing numbers to crowd the land through fragmenting family holdings. The capitalist farmers employed as many workers as it paid them to take on at the going wage rate. Increasing population created a 'supply of labour' for industry to employ.

In England, with foreign trade highly developed under the protection of conquest in India, merchant capital had been amassed in great amounts.

Finally, the social system in England was dominated by an aristocracy and was highly status conscious, yet at the same time ranks were not entirely rigid. It was worthwhile to make money to build up a position that could counter the pretensions of ancient lineage.

[2] See Tobias Dantzig, *Number, the language of science*, p. 33.

Perhaps this last was the chief ingredient lacking in China. China had long been ahead of Europe in all useful arts. A merchant class was well established and an embryonic factory system had grown up here and there.[3] But ambition and intellectual energy went into studying the classics as a means to rise. However that may be, it was in England not in China that the spark fell.

The spark that fell upon all this tinder was the trade in cotton textiles. Merchants were finding a good market for the new commodity, at home because of increased agricultural income, and abroad through sea-borne trade. They found it expedient to begin organizing production instead of merely buying from artisans; from putting out to household workers they developed factories and the employment of labour for wages.

Landless and dispossessed countrymen and artisans ruined by competition from the factories were driven by necessity to become wage-earners.[4] Their disorientation and misery we see repeated today in Asia and Africa where industrialization invades a traditional society.

As now, misery did not prevent numbers from growing, but there was an enormous difference between the population explosion of the nineteenth century and that which is taking place today. Development of the New World, revolutionary improvements in transport and in manufactures to trade for agricultural products, provided an ample supply of food. This is a piece of history that will not repeat itself.

The development of the factory system brought into being a new set of economic and social relationships. The most important was the great expansion of employment at wages. In an economy of peasants and artisans the worker com-

[3] Mark Elvin describes methods of production and 'promotion' in Chinese business in the sixteenth century which have a very modern ring. 'The Failure of Traditional China to Create Industrial Capitalism.' (Unpublished.)

[4] Cf. Christopher Hill 'Pottage for Freeborn Englishmen,' in *Socialism, Capitalism and Economic Growth*, ed. Feinstein,

mands the material factors of production that he operates. Wage labour had swallowed up peasant agriculture in the English system of farming; it was now extended to swallow up artisan manufacture.

It began as pure exploitation – families who had no other means to live could be employed at a subsistence wage and made to work far harder than they would choose to do if they had land or tools of their own. The output could be sold at prices that would undercut the artisan's production and the difference between the wage and the artisan's income accrued as profit to the employer.

The spread of employment brought a corresponding expansion of investment to equip factories and furnish money capital to pay wages and purchase raw materials in advance of sales. (It was from this that the system took the name of capitalism.) The capitalist employer needed energy, ambition and business acumen. These very qualities led him to transcend pure exploitation. With a given method of production there is a limit to the profit that can be got per man employed. By raising output per head, profit could be increased; capitalism quickly set technical progress on foot.

It was here that the specific qualities of cotton played a great role. The system had almost come to the boil with woollens a century before but wool is not so uniform and so amenable to standardized production as cotton; and at the prevailing level of rents and wages, raw cotton per yard of cloth was much cheaper than raw wool, so that it gave much greater scope for profitable manufacture. For long, coal had been mined as a consumption good. Steam power was developed for pumping mines. The application of steam to factory production made coal the source of power. Scientific discoveries were still often made in the pursuit of knowledge for its own sake, but the profit motive provided digestive organs that absorbed them into productive technology. The spiral action of technical development was set going which has been spinning ever since at a more and more vertiginous rate.

From the point of view of the capitalists, the object of the exercise was to make money, but money was needed first and foremost to make money. The successful business-man enlarged his business by ploughing profits back into expansion. His household expenses were kept to a modest share, though they rose to a great level of splendid luxury as the absolute size of the allocation to them grew with the growth of the business.

It was not only superior productivity that caused capitalist wealth to grow. The whole world was ransacked for resources. The dominions overseas that European nations had been acquiring and fighting over since the sixteenth century, and others also, were now greatly developed to supply raw materials to industry. Technical know-how, finance and market outlets enabled the profit seekers to extract animal, mineral and vegetable products from every continent. Labour to exploit them was found in various ways. In the temperate lands peopled mainly from the British Isles, and to some extent in Latin America, local capitalists and local workers (supplemented by continuous immigration) were organized, first by investments of British finance and later from their own accumulation. Wheat, meat, timber, cotton and wool were exchanged partly against profits and interest on the finance that provided transport and other investments to make them available, and partly against imports of manufactures. Minerals had to be found where geology had placed them but vegetable crops such as rubber and tea were moved from one tropical region to another. In Africa labour was recruited by means of imposing taxes so that men had to leave their tribal lands and earn money as wages. The counterpart to mineral exports was almost entirely in profits. In the southern States of USA, the Caribbean and Brazil the labour force had already been provided by the importation of slaves, and emancipation did not make much difference. In Australia slave-trading continued, under the name of blackbirding, by raiding the Pacific islands for manpower but the population to be captured was not adequate. In India, Indonesia, Indo-China and the colonial enclaves on the China coast, needy men in plenty could be recruited for a subsistence wage, and where the local peasantry, as in Ceylon and Malaya, were well enough off, by their own standards, to be able to refuse the indignity, Indians and Chinese were brought in under contract – a form of employment halfway between slavery and wage-earning.

To maintain 'law and order' so as to provide an environment for the creation and extraction of wealth, the capitalist-imperialist nations had to provide an administration in many lands, and this required a number of wars of conquest, but industrial technology had provided them with unchallengeable power, so that it did not cost them much.

At first the demands of workers at home to share in the proceeds of growing productivity were sternly repressed, but gradually combinations developed power; in England, the enlargement of the franchise, humanitarian sentiment and enlightened self-interest of employers led to legislation protecting women and children, a reduction in the hours of work, the spread of education and rising real-wage rates. The employers found that well-fed, literate workers were not only better for producing goods but also constituted a market for selling them. Thus the industrial working class, while apparently struggling against the system, was in fact absorbed into it. (This phenomenon was first noticed in the middle of the nineteenth century in England where Engels remarked, 'This most bourgeois of all nations is apparently aiming ultimately at the possession of a bourgeois aristocracy and a bourgeois proletariat as well as a bourgeoisie.'[5]) This set the pattern followed by successful capitalism everywhere.

The industrial workers at home gained from imperialism in three ways. First of all, raw materials and foodstuffs were cheap relatively to manufactures which maintained the purchasing power of their wages. Tea, for instance, from being a middle-class luxury became an indispensable

[5] *Marx-Engels Correspondence*, p. 115-6.

necessity for the English poor. Secondly the great fortunes made in industry, commerce and finance spilled over to the rest of the community in taxes and benefactions while continuing investment kept the demand for labour rising with the population (though the people of some regions, such as Ireland and the Scottish Highlands, were left to depend upon emigration to find a livelihood). Finally, lording it around the world as members of the master nations, they could feed their self-esteem upon notions of racial superiority.

The chief beneficiaries of the system, of course, were the middle classes. Just as the expenditure of rent nurtured artisans, traders, bureaucrats and learned men, so profits upon an incomparably larger scale called into being new professions of engineers, accountants and dealers in credit, and enlarged the scope of old ones; artists, artisans and tradesmen could flourish in catering to the tastes of the wealthy.

Moreover, the demands of industry for finance (as well as the development of the National Debt) provided boundless scope for lending money at interest. This was further developed with the institution of limited liability, which permitted any owner of wealth to take shares in a company, entitling him to receive profits, without any other responsibilities. This system led to a gradual divorce between nominal ownership in capitalist firms and actual control of them; more and more shares came to be held by owners of wealth acquired by saving or inheritance who had no contact with the businesses concerned, for the great attraction of shares was precisely that they did not tie an individual holder to the bricks or steel which were attracting the profits, but could always be sold on the Stock Exchange when he needed cash or feared that their price was going to fall. They became in effect a kind of rentier property. The original conception was that by this means savings would be channelled into the finance of industry, but the greater part of the business of a stock exchange is in second-hand dealings in paper representing finance that was invested long ago. Since the price of a share depends very much upon the prospects of the firm concerned, or rather on what the market believes about its prospects, fortunes can be made by picking winners without contributing anything to the finance of industry at all. An important group of middle-class professions grew up around this branch of business.

The exaltation of making money for its own sake to respectability, indeed to dominance, in society was the new feature of the capitalist system which distinguished it from all former civilizations. A temperamental inclination to avarice or generosity is no doubt distributed statistically in much the same way in all human populations. There is no reason to suppose that the natural passions were changed in the nineteenth century. Rather a society developed in which ambition and love of power could be satisfied by accumulating wealth, and this met with technical and historical conditions which enabled it to grow and flourish and stretch its tentacles over the world.

The racial concept of class – the inherent superiority of a land-owning family over the tenants and labourers – was undermined by the new wealth. In England it lingered on. The Victorian novels are concerned with the right of the professional classes to consider themselves gentlemen, and gentlemen could not be concerned with trade. Even forty years ago this sentiment was still strong. It was the last lingering remnant of feudal morality – the notion that status was something inborn that could not be bought. Deprived of divine right, the capitalists had to present themselves as benefactors to society. They 'gave employment', they built up the wealth of the nation and carried Christian civilization to barbarous lands. While prosperity lasted they could dismiss all who questioned their credentials as idealists and cranks.

Ever since the cousins of the apes had learned to talk, they explained the world in which they found themselves in terms of spirits and gods. Each of the great religions that developed in the pre-industrial civilizations provided an explanation of the world and of individual life and death combined with moral teaching, a vehicle for mystical contemplation and a system of rituals to give form and grace to daily life. During the nineteenth century the underground of intellectual scepticism which probably always existed and had been growing ever since the revival of Greek speculative thought in the Renaissance, broke surface with the spread of scientific knowledge, in particular with Darwin's recognition that man was a species of animal. (The human psychology that found satisfaction in religion does not seem to have altered but attempts to revive the other aspects of religion without its intellectual content do not appear to be very successful.) With the decay of belief in individual immortality the concept of Progress came to provide the ideology suitable to the system of industrial capitalism.

This has two branches. When capitalism was first getting into its stride Ricardo tried to penetrate its meaning in terms of what we should now call a 'model'.

'The produce of the earth – all that is derived from its surface by the united application of labour, machinery, and capital, is divided among three classes of the community; namely, the proprietor of the land, the owner of the stock or capital necessary for its cultivation, and the labourers by whose industry it is cultivated.

'But in different stages of society, the proportions of the whole produce of the earth which will be allotted to each of these classes, under the names of rent, profit, and wages, will be essentially different; depending mainly on the actual fertility of the soil, on the accumulation of capital and population, and on the skill, ingenuity, and instruments employed in agriculture.

'To determine the laws which regulate this distribution, is the principal problem in political economy.'[6]

[6] David Ricardo, *Principles of Political Economy*, Preface.

The capitalists employed labour at a subsistence wage and rented land. Competition between them set rents at a level that equalized costs of production on better and worse land. The excess of production per man employed, net of rent, over the wage constituted profits. The landlords, inheritors of feudal traditions, consumed their rents; the capitalists saved the greater part of their profit to invest in expanding employment and production. Ricardo advocated changes in law and policy which would play into the hands of the capitalists – in particular, free import of wheat – which would lower the level of rents and encourage accumulation. Pro-capitalist policies triumphed and accumulation bounded ahead.

Marx saw a clue to the interpretation of history in this adaptation of the 'relations of production' – in particular the system of employing labour for profit – to the 'forces of production' – the technical possibilities of the industrial system which was 'raising the productive power of social labour as though in a hothouse'. Imbued with Hegelian notions of rationality, he saw the succession of economic systems as an adaptation of society to the requirements of technology. He concluded that the process of accumulation under the control of the profit motive was a phase which would fulfil itself and come to an end; just as the bourgeoisie had taken over from the aristocracy so the industrial workers would take over from the bourgeoisie and make use of the productive capacity that capitalism created to meet their material needs in a rational manner.

'The monopoly of capital becomes a fetter upon the mode of production, which has sprung up and flourished along with, and under it. Centralization of the means of production and socialization of labour at last reach a point where they become incompatible with their capitalist integument. The integument is burst assunder. The knell of capitalist private property sounds. The expropriators are expropriated.'[7]

[7] *Capital*, Vol. I, Chapter XXXII.

These notions naturally did not appeal to the industrialists and financiers, nor to the thick layers of middle-class rentiers and professionals which were growing up between them and the industrial wage-earners. A more congenial version of the doctrine of progress was put out by Marshall. Through the profit system, the love of money was being harnessed to the service of society. Market demand guided production so that the needs and tastes of the consumers were catered for. Economies of scale and technical progress were reducing costs of production, and competition ensured that prices fell with costs, so that real wages were rising. The spread of education was eroding class differences; any family with the strength of mind to 'forgo present gratifications' by saving could claim a share of profit.

'The problem of social aims takes on new forms in every age : but underlying all there is the one fundamental principle : viz. that progress mainly depends on the extent to which the strongest, and not merely the highest, forces of human nature can be utilized for the increase of social good. There are some doubts as to what social good really is; but they do not reach far enough to impair the foundations of this fundamental principle. For there has always been a substratum of agreement that social good lies mainly in that healthful exercise and development of faculties which yields happiness without pall, because it sustains self-respect and is sustained by hope. No utilization of waste gases in the blast furnace can compare with the triumph of making work for the public good pleasurable in itself, and of stimulating men of all classes to great endeavours by other means than that evidence of power which manifests itself by lavish expenditure. We need to foster fine work and fresh initiative by the warming breath of the sympathy and appreciation of those who truly understand it; we need to turn consumption into paths, that strengthen the consumer and call forth the best qualities of those who provide for consumption. Recognizing that some work must be done that is not ennobling, we must seek to apply the growing knowledge and material resources of the world to reduce such work within narrow limits, and to extirpate all conditions of life which are in themselves debasing. There cannot be a great sudden improvement in man's conditions of life; for he forms them as much as they form him, and he himself cannot change fast : but he must press on steadfastly towards the distant goal where the opportunities of a noble life may be accessible to all.'[8]

It is strange that Marshall published these words in 1919.[9] He was too old to notice that his pleasing prediction had been falsified. In Germany capitalism developed before feudalism had been displaced from agriculture, and feudal notions of war as the natural path to honour had not succumbed to the morality of a nation of shopkeepers. The industrialists looked to the military to win them a share in the wealth of the world and the military encouraged the application of industrial technique to the production of arms. The quick victory of 1870 seemed to vindicate this formula. The capitalist democracies were dragged into an arms race and war which radically changed the nature of the system. Capitalist imperialism, of course, had depended upon military power, but it was turned only against peoples at a much lower technical level who were easily overcome. (The British, indeed, largely used Indian manpower for the little wars that enlarged and maintained the system, and put the greater part of the expense onto the Indian budget.) War between industrial powers was a very different matter. Ever since, the application of scientific technology to means of destruction, each war starting a little above the level at which the last ended, has changed Marshall's agreeable vision of industry at the service of mankind into a nightmare of terror.

[8] Marshall, *Industry and Trade*, pp. 664–5.
[9] Though they were first written much earlier.

7

INTERLUDE OF CONFUSION

LOOKING back in 1938, Professor John Hicks remarked: 'One cannot repress the thought that perhaps the whole Industrial Revolution of the last two hundred years has been nothing else but a vast secular boom.'[1]

A boom in this sense is a situation in which businesses, under the influence of expectations of profit, have brought about a rise in the rate of investment in construction, equipment and stocks.

Investment requires that men are employed and incomes earned in producing goods which will contribute to making profits in the future. Meanwhile they are not bringing anything to market. Incomes currently paid out in connection with them represent demand for goods already available and provide profits for businesses which can supply them. There is a 'seller's market' when demand has increased ahead of capacity to meet it. An initial rise in expenditure on investment thus raises the level of profits and makes further investment attractive. A boom is thus a self-contradictory situation. Investment is stimulated by profits which are generated by the investment itself. When the new capacity which investment has been creating comes into use it competes with the old, the seller's market comes to an end, future prospects of profit are dimmed, new schemes of investment are insufficient to take the place of those that have been completed, and a fall in employment and incomes takes place.

Capitalist industrialization set going one boom after another, to open new territories and exploit new inventions. Each major burst of investment was followed by a recession but new profitable opportunities were always opening up.

[1] Hicks, *Value and Capital*, p. 302, note.

Recessions were only a temporary lull in a continuous
increase of employment and accumulation of wealth. Hick's
suggestion that this was *just* a secular boom means that it
was not a rational self-regulating process, that it depended
uoon an historical accident that was unlikely to repeat itself.
This view reflects the experience of the great slump of the
Thirties.

The slump also can be seen as an historical accident, an
accumulation of tinder into which a spark fell.

The war had speeded up a tendency that was in any case
developing for a number of countries to set up industries
to supply their own needs and reduce their dependence
upon exports from the already developed economies, thus
reduplicating productive capacity, and there had been a
wave of technical improvements in the production of raw
materials which increased supply ahead of demand. The
capitalist world as a whole was sinking into the condition
of a buyer's market. But in the United States, after a post-
war boom and slump, a strong surge of investment set in.
Investment, consumption and national income were rising
more or less continuously from 1921 to 1929 – an excep-
tionally long wave of prosperity which gave rise to the
notion that America was different – that this was not a
mere boom but a new age. There were some signs that the
industrial expansion was beginning to flatten out in 1929,
but the reaction would not have been so violent if it had
not been for the financial boom.

The prices of shares on the Stock Exchange depends, as
we saw above, upon what the market expects them to be.
There had been a sharp post-war boom in reconverting
industry to civilian uses, followed by a sharp slump, which
brought share prices down. Then investment picked up and
the earning power of the real assets which shares represented
was steadily rising. A revaluation of shares began which at
first corresponded to a sober calculation of expected profits.
But soon the Stock Exchange boom took off on its own and
soared away far above the industrial boom.

'Until the beginning of 1928, even a man of conservative mind could believe that the prices of common stock were catching up with the increase in corporation earnings, the prospect for further increases, the peace and tranquillity of the times, and the certainty that the Administration then firmly in power in Washington would take no more than necessary of any earnings in taxes. Early in 1928, the nature of the boom changed. The mass escape into make-believe, so much a part of the true speculative orgy, started in earnest. It was still necessary to reassure those who required some tie, however tenuous, to reality. . . .

'However, the time had come, as in all periods of speculation, when men sought not to be persuaded of the reality of things but to find excuses for escaping into the new world of fantasy.'[2]

'The collapse in the stock market in the autumn of 1929 was implicit in the speculation that went before. The only question concerning that speculation was how long it would last. Sometime, sooner or later, confidence in the short-run reality of increasing common stock values would weaken. When this happened, some people would sell, and this would destroy the reality of increasing values. Holding for an increase would now become meaningless; the new reality would be falling prices. There would be a rush, pell-mell, to unload. This was the way past speculative orgies had ended. It was the way the end came in 1929. It is the way speculation will end in the future.'[3]

The boom meanwhile had been undermining its own base. In an earlier phase there had been a fashion in the U.S.A. for buying foreign bonds. This had supported investment in a number of countries, particularly Germany, where it made it possible to finance reparations payments without building up a corresponding surplus of exports and to carry on investment at home. The attraction of speculation on

[2] J. K. Galbraith, *The Great Crash*, pp. 23–4.
[3] ibid., p. 152–3.

Wall Street dried up the source of foreign loans and brought several countries into financial difficulties. Great Britain had been in chronic trouble, exacerbated by returning to the gold standard at an over-valued exchange rate.[4] The crisis of 1931 brought some relief in the end, but meanwhile unemployment continued to grow. Australia and Latin America were feeling the effects of the sagging prices of primary products, which, as soon as industrial activity slackened, fell to ruinous levels. Thus there was no resiliance anywhere, and the American slump plunged the whole capitalist world into a steep decline of profits, activity and employment.

The doctrines of sound finance, according to which the first duty of a government is to balance its budget, were the dominant orthodoxy, especially in Germany, which had suffered the traumatic experience of a complete breakdown of the monetary system in the great inflation of 1921-3. A change in economic theory which came to be known as the Keynesian Revolution (though Myrdal and Kalecki should share in the ascription[5]), was too late to have any practical effect, and Roosevelt's New Deal was confused and inadequate. Leaving aside misery and humiliation, the waste of mere material production is illustrated by the fact that the outbreak of war increased *civilian* consumption in the United States of food and clothing by about 30 per cent.

It seemed as though Marx's diagnosis was coming true, that capitalism had had its day and was due to be superseded, but history still had more tricks up its sleeve.

A new formula had been found in Italy. When a labour

[4] See J. M. Keynes, *The Economic Consequences of Mr Winston Churchill*. This title is rather unfair as Churchill, the Chancellor of the Exchequer at the time, was obliged to accept advice which he greatly distrusted; see also D. E. Moggridge, *The Return to Gold*, 1925. (Department of Applied Economics, Cambridge, Occasional Paper 19.)

[5] See Gunnar Myrdal, *Monetary Equilibrium*, and Michal Kalecki, *Studies in the Theory of Business Cycles*, both of which (in their own languages) antedate Keynes' *General Theory*.

movement was strong enough to be a serious threat to
landlords and industrialists, the lower middle class of shopkeepers, white collar workers and struggling professionals
felt themselves to be between two fires. They found a
champion who discovered that it was possible to recruit
an army of malcontents and by indulging and cultivating
the sadism that, it seems, is available in every population,
to set up an apparatus of terror to secure power. The
respectable classes were partly intimidated and partly grate-
ful for defence against a revolution from the left. Similarly,
the respectable capitalist nations, through a mixture of fear
and sympathy, allowed the new régime to have its head.
Hitler set out to follow this formula in Germany. The
present misery of massive unemployment and the nagging
bitterness of past defeat provided support for him and he
set about to deal with both at once by preparing for war.

Meanwhile, history had been playing a trick on Marx.
The international labour movement that should have
opposed international capitalism fell apart when the workers
of each nation lined up behind their governments in 1914
with fervent patriotism. But the collapse of the ramshackle
autocracy of the Tsar in the war gave the believers in
Marxism their opportunity and they found themselves in
command of an empire where capitalism, far from being
overripe and rotting from within, had scarcely begun to
take root. It turned out that socialism was not a stage
beyond capitalism but an alternative means of carrying
out industrialization.

After some fumbling about[6] the Soviet authorities
realized that their task was to industrialize the economy
that had come into their hands. Without capitalists to do
the job and the profit motive to guide them, the State had
to develop new organs for the planning and administration
of all economic activities. Within twenty years, the U.S.S.R.

[6] See E. H. Carr, 'Some Random Reflections on Soviet
Industrialization', in *Socialism, Capital and Economic Growth*, ed.
Feinstein.

had overtaken the greater part of the investment which had been accumulating in the Western world over 200 years.

In this the new system had certain advantages. First and foremost, technology had been pioneered under the impulse of the search for profit and had only to be adapted to new requirements. Capitalism had begun from the market, underselling artisan production, and gradually worked back to basic industries. In the new system it was logical to build up the basic industries first and take a short cut through the process of accumulation. The profit motive had grown out of private property. The households of the capitalists demanded to consume a share of profits, which deflected resources from investment. Moreover a great apparatus of credit and finance was developed mainly to deal with property, and this, with salesmanship and advertising, absorbed a large part of the brain power of the capitalist world in unproductive activities. This wastage of the investable surplus could be avoided by organizing an administration to do only what was necessary to keep the economy running.

In the capitalist world there was a sharp division between goods and services to be provided by the state and those to be provided by private enterprise. Everything that could be sold in packets or charged for by a fee was an opportunity to make profits. General administration and the armed forces, and some urban amenities, had to be paid for out of taxes. (At first even roads were provided on the profit system, but since tolls were clearly too much of a nuisance this service was transferred to the tax sector.)

Taxes are felt to be a burden, if not outright robbery, while profits concealed in the prices of goods are not. The public generally accepted the ideology of the businessmen and supported them in keeping the market sphere as wide as possible. As productivity increased, even the lowest incomes offered a market for more and more goods of mass production, but the most important services – health and education – could be adequately supplied only to the middle class families that could pay for them. In the Soviet system the distinction between taxes and profits does not arise. The whole of the fund required to pay the incomes of those engaged in the administration, the armed forces, investment and free services are collected together and expended on a coherent plan. The provision of health and education services is extended to the whole population, which besides its contribution to the standard of life, has the advantage of allowing the industrial system to draw upon the talents of the whole of every generation.

There is another drawback about the tax system in the capitalist countries. Democratic sentiment demands that income from property, which is permanent, should be taxed more heavily than income from work which falls off in sickness and old age; and it demands that high incomes should at least appear to be heavily taxed. The result is that ingenuity and lawyers' fees spent upon avoiding tax often brings a higher return than can be earned by contributing to real production.

'One element of these costs should be mentioned specifically. It consists in the absorption of ability in merely protective activities. A considerable part of the total work done by lawyers goes into the struggle of business with the state and its organs. It is immaterial whether we call this vicious obstruction of the common good or defence of the common good against vicious obstruction. In any case the fact remains that in socialist society there would be neither need nor room for this part of legal activity. The resulting saving is not satisfactorily measured by the fees of lawyers who are thus engaged. That is inconsiderable. But not inconsiderable is the social loss from such unproductive employment of many of the best brains. Considering how terribly rare good brains are, their shifting to other employments might be of more than infinitesimal importance.'[7]

[7] Joseph A. Schumpeter, *Capitalism, Socialism and Democracy*, p. 198.

The Russian Revolution abolished income from property (apart from a small amount of interest on savings) and income tax is applied only to a few anomalous cases. For the great bulk of the active population, each individual receives the income that he is supposed to have. There is no need for an elaborate organization to pay out money with one hand and take it back with another.

When private property in the means of production has been abolished the whole national income belongs to the whole population. The earnings of a worker are not wages in the same sense as under capitalism; they are his share in the grand co-operative enterprise. However, as a means of enforcing discipline and providing a motive for work, a system of payments indistinguishable from wages proved indispensable; socialism made much less difference to the daily life of an industrial worker than the visionaries had promised. For the manager of an enterprise life *was* different. Instead of being called upon to use his judgment as to how to make profits for his firm, he was given instructions in the form of specifications of output, costs, etc. in terms of which he had to make the best showing that he could.

The most important difference in the economy that socialism introduced was in the control of investment. Instead of being divided by historical accident between government, local authorities, a number of profit-seeking large scale enterprises and innumerable little businesses making a livelihood for a family, with no generally accepted view of what it was supposed to be for, an overall plan of investment to build up the strength of the nation was now the main preoccupation of the central government.

The planners had at their command great untapped natural resources and a large part of their task was to organize the production of raw materials. An overall plan required a balance of the supply of each kind of animal, vegetable and mineral product against its use in construction and manufactures. A system of planning was evolved in terms of physical inputs and outputs and an administrative system for implementing the plan developed through the allocation to enterprises of materials, power and a wage fund to recruit labour. This system was set to work to modernize and industrialize the whole empire inherited from the Tsars at the most rapid possible rate. A system without 'capital' in the sense of private property in finance proved highly successful in accumulating 'capital' in the sense of industrial equipment.

But there were certain serious drawbacks in the Soviet system. First, industrialization was launched before the agricultural revolution which had preceded it in the Western world.

In the course of the Revolution and the civil war in which it was established, the peasants in Russia had taken possession of the land; and in central Asia, tribal leaders had resumed their ancient powers. Rent, which formerly syphoned off the agricultural surplus, was not being paid, and, while industry could offer nothing to buy, the peasants had no motive to produce a surplus for sale. Stalin cut his way through this impasse by setting up collective farms, servicing them with machine-tractor stations which were intended to boost production, and requiring compulsory deliveries of grain and other crops. The murderous brutality with which the collectivization was carried out alienated the peasants, and few of the managers sent to run the farms could find a way to make them work. (In the Asian Republics, when the chieftains had been subdued, the new system brought a rise of the standard of life above its former miserable level and so enlisted support.) The poor performance of agriculture set a serious drag upon the development of Soviet industry.

The second great drawback of the system was that the faith which made the revolution possible became hardened into dogma. Marx-Leninism (far from the intentions of its authors) became an obscurantist, persecuting religion. Physics and engineering were too important to be smothered, but questions of biology, linguistics, psychology, aesthetics, and, above all, economics and social science, were settled by decree. The contradiction between the wide spread of education, particularly in natural science, and the prohibition of a free intellectual life of inquiry and criticism set up a tension which has not yet been resolved.

Finally, being surrounded by the hostility of the capitalist nations, which treated even Fascism as a lesser evil, the Soviet government was obliged to gear industry primarily to defence and to keep a sharp eye on internal dissent. To carry through the whole programme required strong central control, which hypertrophied into the tyranny of Stalin. The relations of production were adjusted to fit the forces of production with a painful wrench.

In the end, Hitler made the Russians and the West into allies, but when the war was over the old hostility reasserted itself and the era of the Cold War began.

8

INDUSTRY AND STATE

AFTER the war, capitalism was found to have undergone an important mutation. The boom of post-war reconstruction was not followed by a post-reconstruction slump. For more than twenty years there was no major recession. How long this new epoch will last no one can tell, but it has already lasted long enough to appear as a new phase in industrial civilization.

The predominant element in the capitalist world is now the United States and it is there that we must look for the mechanism of the new system. There were two main elements in it, playing into each other's hands. First, the era of personal capitalism, when the 'robber barons' built up large fortunes, had come to an end (though some areas for wheeling and dealing still remain). They were succeeded by great bureaucratized concerns adapted to the application of scientific methods to technology, management and salesmanship. Second, the greatly enlarged concern of the State in economic affairs, which had begun in the slump and grown in the war, continued into quasi-peacetime.

The great corporations inherited the aims and attitudes individual capitalists but there are important differences in their mode of operation. Once launched they do not depend for finance upon individual saving. Each consists in a self-perpetuating and self-expanding fund controlled and serviced by a self-perpetuating cadre of managers and technicians.

The technostructure, as Galbraith has chistened it, consists of 'all who bring specialized knowledge, talent or experience to group decision-making'.[1] No individual has more power than a cog in a machine, but the machine as

---

[1] *The New Industrial State*, p. 71.

a whole controls an empire of millions of money and thousands of lives.

There is a strong propensity in human nature – perhaps rooted in the instincts which give social cohesion to a company of apes – to develop loyalty to whatever institution an individual finds himself in. Managerial capitalism requires a high degree of attachment of the staff to a corporation. Self-interest, of course, is involved but pure self-interest would lead to great mobility between businesses and the disclosure of the secrets of one to another. Loyalty which invests the ego of the individual in his corporation is an essential feature of the system.

It is no-one's business to ask 'What is the object of the operation?' To the servants of each corporation it seems natural and obvious that they should be working for the success of the business. Nominally the management of a concern is employed by its owners and the legal owners of it are the shareholders (stockholders). But the shareholders – individual rentiers, insurance companies and so forth – have no say in the conduct of the business; they regard their claims merely as placements, a convenient form of holding and drawing income from property. The managers are continually striving to increase profits by investments which reduce costs so as to improve their selling power. This makes it possible for real wages to rise without reducing the rate of profit. The major part of this investment is financed out of profits and the earning power of the capital so created is the property of whoever happens to be holding the shares. Thus the position of the stockholder is anomalous.

'He is a passive and functionless figure, remarkable only in his capacity to share, without effort or even without appreciable risk, in the gains from the growth by which the technostructure measures its success. No grant of feudal privilege has ever equalled, for effortless return, that of the grandparent who bought and endowed his descendants with a thousand shares of General Motors or General Electric.

The beneficiaries of this foresight have become and remain rich by no exercise of effort or intelligence beyond the decision to do nothing, embracing as it did the decision not to sell.'[2]

This system ensures for the managements a high degree of independence from bankers and governments and for that reason they tolerate the drain on the firm's resources represented by the necessity to pay out enough dividends to secure its good standing on the Stock Exchange.

The capitalism of the great corporations has proved itself to be ideally designed for applying the discoveries of the physical sciences to production and the discoveries of psychology and social research to creating demands for its products, but it could not by itself manage the national economy.

There is an ever-rising consumption of industrial products by the middle class of farmers, small businesses, professionals including the personnel of the technostructure itself, and that part of the working class which had become absorbed into the system; the system has come to be known as the 'consumer society'. But this is not a sufficient base to provide an outlet for the sheer mass of investible funds which the system generates. Moreover the inherent instability of investment which the private enterprise economy had manifested before the war is now coupled with a potential instability in consumption. (If everyone decided to run his car for another year, modern industry, not only in America, would be plunged into a dreadful slump.)

The system *has* however kept running with only moderate fluctuations. State expenditure has provided a balancing element in demand to preserve near-stability and continuous growth in the market for goods. The easiest line of expenditure for the state to undertake is for so-called defence.

'It provides contracts of long duration, calling for large investment of capital in areas of advanced technology.

[2] ibid., p. 394.

There is no risk of price fluctuations. There is full protection against any change in requirements, i.e. any change in demand. Should a contract be cancelled the firm is protected on the investment it has made. For no other products can the technostructure plan with such certainty and assurance. Given the inevitability of planning, there is much attraction in circumstances were it can be done so well.

'This leads the technostructure to identify itself closely with the goals of the armed services and, not infrequently, with the specific goals of the particular service, Army, Navy or Air Force, which it most intimately serves. Simple association, as in the case of individual and organization, supports this tendency. In consequence the technostructure, comes to see the same urgency in weapons development, the same security in technical pre-eminence, the same requirement for a particular weapons system, the same advantage in an enlarged mission for (say) the Air Force or Navy, as does the particular service itself. Its members develop the same commitment to these goals as do officers of the services.'[8]

There may have been some far-sighted government advisors who saw the arms race as a solution of the problem of maintaining economic stability, but it seems plausible to suppose that this formula came from a convergence of a variety of forces. The military and all the authorities who had risen to positions of power and honour in the war were reluctant to step down. A number of important industries would have suffered a sharp decline if armaments production had fallen off; the scientists who had committed themselves to the atom bomb did not want to believe that it was unnecessary; politicians, financiers and industrialists feared that sympathy with the Russian people might encourage communism at home; broad masses of white workers, small businessmen, members of the technostructure and intellectuals still held the faith propounded by Al Capone : 'This

[8] ibid., pp. 310–11,

American system of ours . . . gives to each and everyone
of us a great opportunity if we only seize it with both
hands'[4] and were ready to rally round at any suggestion
that it was in danger.

Whatever its causes, the consequence of the Cold War
was to provide an outlet for government expenditure which
did not compete with private enterprise and which did not
saturate demand by producing anything that the public
could consume.

The system was quickly recognized :

'The Government planners figure they have found the
magic formula for almost endless good times . . . *Cold War*
is the catalyst. Cold War is an automatic pump primer.
Turn a spigot, the public clamors for more arms spending.
Turn another, the clamor ceases. Truman confidence,
cockiness, is based on this "Truman formula". *Truman era
of good times*, the President is told, can run much beyond
1952. Cold War demands, if fully exploited, are almost
limitless.'[5]

The vested interest of all who depend for profits or employment on the arms industry (including a large proportion of
the universities and research institutes) gave it a solid
backing, and the crusade for 'freedom' gave it a noble aim.

This system has proved itself remarkably successful, not
for fighting wars, but for maintaining continuous profitability and so permitting a continuous growth of industry,
which, so to speak as a by-product, could continuously
expand the output and consumption of marketable goods.
The relations of production were better adapted to the forces
of scientific technology than ever before. Living in the era
that came to an end in 1914, Marx had supposed that there
was necessarily a kind of rationality in such an adaptation;
now the opposite appears. Atomic, chemical and biological

[4] See below p. 116.
[5] Quoted from U.S. News and World Report in Baran and
Sweezy, *Monopoly Capital*, p. 212.

weaponry have not only finally destroyed war as a scene of bravery and honour, they have made it too dangerous to provide a means of national aggrandisement. Rationality requires that the prime aim of policy should be to make war obsolete and to find alternative ways of dealing with the problems that give rise to it; but it is precisely the economic success of the military-industrial complex (though it has over-reached itself in Vietnam) that puts the greatest obstacle in the way of any such attempt.

To maintain near-full employment, it is not enough merely to preserve stability. It is necessary also to ensure that the number of jobs that the economy offers grows at the same pace as the working population. Technical progress is continually reducing the number of man-hours of work required, this year, to produce last year's output. At the same time, when the population is growing, greater numbers are seeking employment this year than last. To prevent unemployment requires the demand for labour to rise along with the supply.

An adequate rate of increase of total output together with a reduction in man-hours of work per man-year and a lengthening of the period of education enables the system to digest technical change which is gradual and widely diffused throughout industry, though there does not seem much logic in allowing the 'passive and functionless' shareholder to enjoy a large part of the benefit. But the profit motive contains no mechanism to ensure that technical progress will take digestible forms.

The mechanization of agriculture in the ex-slave states of USA, combined with automation in industry and the atrophy of public transport, has made a large part of the unskilled labour force redundant to the requirements of profitable industry. The concentration of the consequent unemployment on black people is creating a horrifying problem.

Modern capitalism is well adapted to produce fabulous technical successes, but not to provide the basis for the noble life accessible to all that Marshall dreamed of.

9

THE NEW MERCANTILISM

CAPITALISM with near-full employment proved highly
successful also in Western Europe. While armaments provided the flywheel that kept the market economy steady,
the most spectacular development was seen in the defeated
nations, West Germany and Japan (for Japan is now part
of the 'Western world' of capitalist industry), which were
at first not allowed to recreate their military industry and
so put all their investment and all their injured national
pride into civilian production. Even in Great Britain, the
least successful practitioner of modern capitalism, there was
a marked rise in the level of consumption of industrial
products, and the destruction of amenities that accompanies
it.

An important by-product of capitalist prosperity was a
great expansion of the system of social services that had
been pioneered in Great Britain at the beginning of the
century and greatly developed in emulation of the Soviets.
In this the demands of democracy and humanitarian sentiment combined with the enlightened self-interest of the
business community. A destitute citizen is a reproach to
the economy and of no use to it as a worker to produce, or
a market to absorb, saleable goods; ill-health is wasteful
and public education is necessary to produce skilled workers
and the lower echelons of the technostructure. Thus modern
capitalism takes a turn towards the welfare state.

This system has been carried furthest in Sweden, where
war had been avoided. The other nations seek to excuse
themselves from lagging behind by putting it about that
the Swedes are terribly bored.

Gunnar Myrdal the distinguished Swedish economist and
sociologist, describes this as bunk.[1]

[1] 'What is wrong with the Welfare State?' *New York Times
Sunday Magazine*, January 30, 1966.

'Sweden has succeeded in establishing an economy in which mass unemployment is disappearing from the horizon; there is an increasingly effective public service for aiding those individuals in danger of becoming unemployed in a lagging industry, so that even the exceptional unemployment risk is reduced; all citizens in case of illness have at their disposal medical facilities for only a nominal fee; they can look forward to a pension in old age that, in stable value, will amount to two-thirds of their income in their best fifteen years; decent living standards are guaranteed by the state for children, widows, invalids, and handicapped; by law it is forbidden to dismiss a woman for family reasons; women in public service before and after childbirth are given paid leave from employment and all women are compensated for various costs relating to the event; all schools are free and the students and their families also are gradually relieved from the necessity of finding support for their living costs; strenuous efforts are made to help families in modest circumstances to get a decent home to live in; and so on.'[2]

One piece of supposed evidence of the frustration and sadness of the Swedes is the statistics of suicide, which are higher than those of some other countries largely because suicide there is not a crime and is not reported in newspapers, so that families have no reason to hush it up.

'Another popular idea abroad is the prevalence of 'sin' in Sweden, meaning sexual freedom. One moot point is, to begin with, how this type of 'sin' could bear testimony of frustration and sadness.'[3]

Myrdal, who has been used to playing a role on the world stage, confesses that he is rather bored himself in a society where there are no large problems, but most of his countrymen seem to find it quite satisfactory.

[2] ibid. A small verbal change has been made in the quotation.
[3] ibid.

'Undoubtedly, the rise in material welfare and security for the masses has not been accompanied by the sharp improvement of cultural participation which we believed should result from the social reforms at the time when we had to fight for them. We certainly believed, for instance, that four weeks' paid vacation should come to be put to somewhat other uses than for what we now can observe they are commonly used. But that was a mistake in our analysis of things to come. Least of all should it be taken as showing malaise among the people. Apparently, they are not so keen on higher culture, as we romantically believed, but are quite happy with a small, though rising share in it.[4]

It is possible to argue that in Sweden democratic public opinion has mastered the industrialists and made them its servants, while in USA the state has become the servant of the industrialists. Other Western countries lie somewhere in between.

When it is the accepted aim of government policy to preserve near-full employment and 'economic growth', which satisfies national self-respect and keeps a democracy contented by permitting the majority of its citizen a rising level of consumption, then clearly the management of industrial firms and the trade unions are just as much a part of the administration of the national economy as the Civil Service; at the same time democracy has no direct means of controlling them; they have to be cajoled and offered inducements, or threatened with prohibitions, to get them to do what the aims of policy require. Each of the capitalist nations has evolved a different pattern of relationships between government, nationalized industries and services, and private enterprise; and a different pattern of distribution of the benefits between classes and sectors of the economy, according to the strength and pretentions of the interests involved.[5] Boring or not, the welfare state has very much softened the harshness of raw capitalism and has

[4] ibid.   [5] See Shonfield, *Modern Capitalism*.

played a large part in saving it, till now, from the doom that Marx foresaw a hundred years ago.

As well as industrial technology, the second ingredient in the high standard of life of the developed nations is birth control. In the eighteenth century even well-to-do women suffered like Mrs Thrale : 'Forever bringing and losing babies which tears the body and the mind so terribly.'[6] Medical improvements brought down the infant death rate and were followed by a limitation of births. A long struggle against prejudice has not yet been completely victorious, but it has been sufficiently successful to bring a revolutionary change in family life in prosperous industrial societies.

The freedom that Myrdal refers to is an adaptation of manners to a new technical situation, though the young generation, beset by a hangover of puritanism on one side and the commercial vulgarization of sex on the other, has a hard time to establish for themselves an acceptable psychological attitude and a practicable code of behaviour.

From the point of view of private life, the acceptance of birth control has been a great liberation, though the fall in birth rates following recent technical and legal improvements in methods shows that there were still a great number of unwanted births. From the point of view of the economy, the movement has not gone far enough. A cessation of growth of numbers in a near-full employment welfare economy would make possible a more rapid rise in the average standard of consumption with less destruction of amenities in space, water and air. All the capitalist industrial nations are still suffering from growing numbers; and the humanitarians are in a cruel dilemma between wanting to rescue all the children who do get born from poverty and fear of encouraging their parents to bear more.

The welfare state, just as much as the needs of 'defence', promotes nationalism. Each government is concerned for its

[6] Quoted from memory from a letter in *Thraliana*.

own people and policy cannot distinguish between benefits to them which are absolute and those which are at the expense of other peoples. As Myrdal points out, the democratic welfare state in the rich countries of the Western world is essentially, by its very nature, protectionist and nationalistic.[7]

The great differences in the standard of life and level of employment in different parts of the world sets up a demand for immigration into the most prosperous economies. So long as immigrants will do the roughest work at the lowest wages, they are helping to raise the standard of life of the natives, but if they settle and share the benefits of the welfare state they become a menace to it. An ideal solution (from the point of view of the native capitalists) has been found in Western Germany where workers from poorer countries are brought in, ready-made with no cost for their rearing, when industry is booming, and expelled when unemployment threatens. In such situations, it is taken for granted that the welfare only of the natives is the concern of the home government, whether the system offers any advantages to foreigners or not.

The national egoism of modern capitalism is clearly seen in the sphere of international trade. The capitalist world (except in a major war) is a buyer's market. Productive capacity exceeds demand. Exports yield profits and imports (apart from necessary raw materials) mean a loss of sales to competitors. Moreover internal investment is easier to foster, inflation easier to fend off and the foreign exchange easier to manage in a situation of a *favourable* balance of trade – that is, an excess of exports over imports. Thus every nation competes to achieve 'export-led growth', while each tries to defend itself from the exports of the others. The combination of national quasi-planning with international chaos (which the agreements on trade and finance made after the war have not succeeded in mastering) flares up from time to time in an international crisis.

[7] See *Beyond the Welfare State*.

The requirements of the warfare state and the welfare state meet in the export of armaments, which keep industry in ex-imperialist countries prosperous and permit enmities in the ex-colonial countries, which were frozen at the level of bows and arrows or flintlocks, to break out with bombs and tanks.

10

SOCIALIST AFFLUENCE

ON the Soviet side, a great part of the accumulation of twenty years was to do again, because of wartime destruction, and on top of this it was more necessary than ever to gear science and industry to defence. A second period of investment at all costs set in. The *de facto* settlement at the end of the war (which has never been regularized) gave the Soviets a sphere of influence in Central Europe up to the Oder-Neiser line and the Balkans except for Greece; Czechoslovakia (perhaps to forestall a movement from the other side) joined in 1947. The Russian system was transplanted into all these countries, including its tyranny and injustice. In spite of all, the powerful effect of planned development has raised production (including armaments) over the whole area to such a level that a policy of relaxation becomes possible and the demands of the public for some benefit from their toil and abstinence become insistent.

The era of potential affluence took the Soviet planners by surprise. During the period of heavy accumulation it was considered to be a 'law of socialism' that the proportion of annual investment devoted to expanding the investment industries should be greater than the proportion devoted to building up capacity in consumer good industries. Thus the proportion of investment in national income should be growing and the rate of accumulation accelerating. It now has to be admitted that this is not a 'law' but a phase of development. When the first phase of industrialization comes to an end the economy can settle down to the rate of growth given by a constant proportion of investment, and this need not be the highest proportion that was reached in the process of acceleration.

During the period of accelerating accumulation, a kind

of anti-consumer ideology was developed by the planners. Only heavy industry was taken seriously. The Soviet system proved to be very efficient for producing sputniks but very inefficient at meeting the housewife's daily needs. Unnecessary hardships were imposed upon the consumer, for instance by failure to provide for services such as repairs for shoes and watches, over and above the hardships necessarily entailed by high accumulation and an economy dominated by defence. The method of controlling industry by commands from above which were often incompatible with each other, the statement of plans in terms of gross output which encouraged a wasteful use of materials, and an arbitrary system of prices, led to inefficiency in production. The economic system which proved successful in applying a forced draft to accumulation was proving to be an impediment to enjoying its fruits. The relations of production had to be adapted to a new situation.

Schemes of reform began to be discussed along with the denunciation of Stalin in 1956. After simmering for ten years, there was a fresh outburst of criticism and experiment. The struggle between new ideas and old authority came to a crisis with a political upheaval in Czechoslovakia in 1968. The Soviet intervention was a sharp set-back to political liberalization and freedom of opinion. It remains to be seen how the economic reforms can function without the open discussion and criticism in which they were conceived.

The reformers are embarking on uncharted seas. They have been influenced to some extent by the account of capitalism which is given in Western textbooks and seem to suppose that 'the market' and 'the maximization of profits' can provide a solution for their problems. There is, certainly, a hump that they can draw upon in the very inefficiency of the old system. By obliging the managers of enterprises to produce goods that will be sold to the public, instead of dumping into the shops planned output that no one wants, there can be an immediate lift in the real purchasing power of the consumer's income. But the textbooks only discuss the use of *given* resources to meet *given* wants. When resources are growing, the consumers do not know what they are going to want until it is offered to them. In the West, particularly in USA, there is a great deal of market research, but it is devoted mainly to finding out the most effective methods of salesmanship and advertisement. An advanced industry which is genuinely devoted to 'securing the maximum satisfaction of the constantly rising material and cultural requirements of the whole society'[1] is something that the world has not yet seen.

The textbook notion that the objective of maximizing the profits of an enterprise ensure efficiency is also very superficial. Even the textbooks nowadays admit that capitalist firms weigh the aim of long-run growth against the aim of short-run profits and that they have to take into account good relations with workers and a good reputation with consumers in deciding upon their policies, so that profitability is not a simple unambiguous criterion of success.

There are obvious advantages in giving the socialist managers simplified instructions. When prices have been rationalized, an instruction in terms of profits makes it possible to cut through the tangle of 'plan indicators' formerly in operation, but it is still by no means clear how it will work out in practice.

The second great problem for the reformers is to engage the loyalty of the workers. In the nature of the case, the reformers belong to the technostructure of socialism – they are educated, intelligent experts and administrators, some within the Communist Party and some without. They feel that it is right and necessary to give the technostructure independence, authority and a reasonable standard of life. They cannot any longer represent revolution as the triumph of the insulted and injured. (In Czechoslovakia, the Russians in 1968 raised a powerful wave of national feeling

[1] See Stalin, *Economic Problems of Socialism in USSR*, p. 45.

against themselves which brought popular support to the reformers.)

In Yugoslavia, which escaped from the grip of Stalinist orthodoxy in 1950, the equity in each enterprise was given to the workers employed in it when the new system was introduced. They appointed their own managers and decided what part of net proceeds should be paid out as wages, used for amenities or invested in improving productive capacity. This had a great success in imbuing the workers on the shop floor with that kind of loyalty to the business which is usual in the higher levels of management, but it very soon disrupted the overall plan within which it was intended to operate. The other reformers are trying to find a way to enlist the energy and good conduct of workers by means of incentive payments while keeping a grip on the management of the economy as a whole. In this respect, also, it remains to be seen what will come out of the reforms in concrete reality.

Perhaps the most important achievement of the Soviet system was the development of public education, far ahead of anything seen in welfare capitalism, and the opening of opportunity to talent for all the peoples of the Union. This was accompanied by a stratification of income and status according to the educational level required for various kinds of work. For a long time the requirements for trained personnel of the administration, industry (including armaments and space travel) and the social services, including education itself, was running ahead of what the system could provide; recently it was found that supply had caught up upon requirements so that there begin to be more qualified candidates than places carrying the privileges which they expected to enjoy. In the severely utilitarian drive for production, the concept of education as an end in itself had been lost. The idea was even suggested of limiting entry to higher education so that there would be a sufficient number of workers obliged to remain in the lower ranks.[2]

[2] See Kyril Tidmarsh, The Times, October 9, 1968.

The emergence of some signs of a 'consumer society' in the Soviet world has led to a discussion in the West of a convergence of the two economic systems. It is true that on the capitalist side there has been a move towards national planning and on the socialist side a move towards making use of market indicators, and it is true that enterprises operating the same techniques have very much the same kind of internal organization. However, the manner in which the two processes of industrialization took place has left important differences.

The problems which the Soviets are meeting in adapting their system to potential affluence are very unlike the problems which beset modern capitalist governments in trying to control private enterprise. Controlled trade may be clumsy and wasteful but a balance of payments problem cannot arise when imports are kept to the level that exports can pay for. The elimination of wage bargaining permits full employment to be maintained without the nuisance of continuously rising money-wage rates and prices. Sudden devastating changes in the demand for labour are avoided by introducing automation no faster than its consequences can be dealt with. The elimination of rentier property (though it has not created a classless society) prevents the drain upon the investable surplus and the distortions of the pattern of demand which are due to the consumption of what our tax collectors neatly describe as 'unearned income'.

On both sides, industrialization took place under the aegis of national governments. The Soviet sphere, in some ways even more than welfare capitalism, is dominated by economic nationalism. The European socialist countries have found it difficult to co-operate in a common plan of development. Trade is controlled mainly by bilateral exchanges which excludes a great deal of the potential advantages of international division of labour and each economy finds itself restricted by limitations on its capacity to import. On the other hand, the sphere of planned trade remains immune to the recurrent crises that beset the capitalist world.

The thesis of convergence is used in the West to mitigate the blind hatred of 'communism' and in China, under the title of 'revisionism', to accuse the Soviets of having abandoned the principles of socialism. But meanwhile the shadow of the Cold War still hangs over the scene. On the one side this allows the authorities to override objections to keeping up the arms race and on the other side allows the authorities to stifle free discussion for fear that criticism may turn into disloyalty.

II

ANOTHER WAY

In China, as in Russia, socialism is proving to be the means to foster accumulation and instil scientific technology in a pre-industrial economy, but there it takes a new form. Under the banner of Marx-Leninism, Mao Tse-tung conceived of a revolution that would be really in the interests of the people. In China the mass of the people were impoverished villagers. To benefit them, the first task of the revolution was the transformation of agriculture.

Immediately after the installation of the People's Republic, a thoroughgoing land reform (which had already been rehearsed in areas taken over during the long civil war) liberated the cultivators from oppression and insecurity, raising the vast majority to the status of a middle peasant, that is, of a family with enough land to utilize their own labour and provide themselves more or less with a living.

But a peasantry at that level could not provide the basis for modern industrial development. Holdings were tiny, tools and animals deficient and technique primitive. To set the spiral going, a surplus had to be passed over to industry which in turn would provide the means to modernize agriculture. Moreover the desperate acquisitiveness of the peasant, so long struggling on the brink of penury, did not fit with the ideals of socialism.

By a series of gradual steps, land was collectivized; by stages, the peasant ceased to be a peasant in formal status and became a team-member in an Agricultural Commune. (There are also some state farms cultivated by wage labour.) In methods of work too, the peasant changed his style of life. The layout of fields and the allocation of tasks was rationalized; investment in water control, breeding of animals, electrification and finally mechanization, raised the level of production per man as well as per acre. (Chinese Communists admit that in the process gross errors were made, but a run of eight years of overall good harvests indicates that they have been pretty well corrected.)

The economic relationships of the peasant have also been transformed. The team has in effect property in the land that has been allotted to it and in the stock that it has acquired, as well as in an accumulation fund and social-welfare fund built up from its earnings. Rent and usury are no more.

The income derived from the produce of the team, in kind and in cash, is distributed according to the work-points that each individual has recorded to his credit. Production is still mainly for self-subsistence. To put it crudely, if 80 per cent of the labour force is engaged in agriculture, they need to part with only 20 per cent of their net produce to feed the rest of the population at the same level as themselves. (Formerly, the exactions of the landlord often took 50 per cent of gross produce.) The surplus is purchased at fixed prices (apart from a land-tax based on notional yields which is ceasing to be of importance as actual yields rise). Each team agrees with the procurement authorities on the quantities to be sold every year. The agreements are intended to leave enough for the team to feed itself, so that the surplus is skimmed off where yields are highest. To make the rural population pleased to earn money, supplies of consumer goods are made available for them to buy.

Finally, in attitude of mind, also, the peasant is ceasing to be a peasant. The young generation that has grown up to think of collective work and collective ownership of the means of production as the normal thing, is losing interest in the private plots which were permitted as a concession to old ways and is mainly concerned with learning new techniques and acquiring new equipment. The range of occupations in the countryside is widening from year to year as mechanization increases and more and more small industries are installed in the Communes. Education and the discussion of politics brings the villager into the swim of national life.

Given complete economic security, at no matter how simple a level, and convincing prospects of future improvement, the ex-peasant can respond to the appeal of the Cultural Revolution : combat egoism and eschew privilege.

For obvious reasons, the development of industry cannot be so different from the Soviet model though human relations in the factory are much more democratic in China, and the Chinese appear to have aroused even greater than Yugoslav enthusiasm for production and technical progress without appealing to monetary incentives.

Chinese planners from the start paid the kind of consideration to the consumer that is only now coming into fashion in the Soviet Union. They avoided getting jammed up in centralized rigidity by a very simple device, that was, to control production and retailing from the wholesale stage.

In the coastal cities a certain number of native capitalists (mainly in textiles) had grown up under the wing of the foreign Concessions. When the cities were liberated, these businesses were encouraged to continue production; they were supplied with materials and their output purchased at fixed prices. This method was extended over the greater part of light industry when it was absorbed into the socialist system. An office of the Ministry of Internal Trade arranges contracts between enterprises at different stages of production (say, supplies from a spinner to a weaver) and between the final producer and the retail shops. The contract governs the product mix, design, delivery dates and prices. The retailer transmits market demands to the office, which modifies contracts for the next period accordingly. Thus the consumer's requirements govern supply instead of the other way round. It is true that mass consumption in China is still at a very simple level, but there seems no reason why this system should not work successfully as it rises. A system of contracts with surrounding communes ensures the supply of meat, fruit and vegetables to the towns and cities.

The most original and striking of Mao's conceptions concerns the relation of the administration and the professions to the simple workers. Mao observed in Russia that status becomes the basis of privilege when property has been abolished and that, through privileged education, it can become hereditary and form the basis for class. A Communist Party organized in the Stalinist tradition creates a gulf between the rulers and the ruled. Moreover, in China millenial tradition exalted learning and despised manual work. The roots of class, in the administration and the professions, remained in the ground after property was cut down, and would soon sprout again.

The drive for political education based on the Thought of Mao Tse-tung is intended to dig out the roots of privilege, make work honourable, level inequalities and establish the right of rank and file to criticize the Party and the administration in each line of activity.

Equality in consumption cannot be established in a poor country. If there are not enough leather shoes for everyone to have a pair, some are wearing leather and some wearing straw. There are great differences between earnings in rich and poor communes, even between a successful and a backward team in one commune. The aim is to approach equality by raising standards from the bottom. Meanwhile, everyone must work so as to learn what work is; education is not to provide the individual with a comfortable niche, but to enable him to 'serve the people' in some particular way; everyone must learn to value himself on what he gives to society, not on what he gets out of it. Thus Chinese socialism aims to solve the dilemma that the Czech reformers ran into, between democracy and individual incentives, by a moral appeal.

In this, past history was an indispensable support. For three thousand years, the slow turnover of the population, in which class was never based on 'race', has soaked them all in Chinese civilization, and Chinese civilization has always been based upon the conception of correct conduct. ('We may be poor people, but we do know right from wrong.') It is much easier to alter the content of correct conduct for people trained in such a view of life than to introduce the concept itself among people imbued with cynicism and grasping competitiveness.

Chinese socialism is something new in the world. The Czech reformers claimed to establish socialism with a human face. The Chinese have set out on the more ambitious course of establishing economic development with a human sense of values. They are still in the glow of a successful revolution, supported by recent memories of the misery and corruption from which they have emerged. Another twenty years will show whether or not humanity is capable of carrying out such a programme.

12

THE THIRD WORLD

Colonies in the original sense of the word are settlements of families from the home country taking root overseas. In imperial dominions a native or imported population is governed by administrators and opened to penetration by businessmen and missionaries who do not become permanent residents. (In British usage, colonies were called Dominions and dominions were called Colonies.)

The areas of British and French settlement in the New World, including the United States, entered the swim of capitalist development. (White settlements in Africa are a special and anomalous case.) The colonies of Spain and Portugal in Latin America developed capitalism with less success and their nations are now classed with the successor states of the British, French and Dutch empires as the underdeveloped economies. (Only the Portuguese in Africa still try to maintain imperial possessions in the old style.)

The concept of 'underdevelopment' arises from the contrast with the 'developed' economies, which are a recent and localized phenomenon. The basic economic characteristic of underdevelopment, which has been the normal state of the world everywhere and in all ages until now, is a low level of output per head of foodstuffs (low by comparison with what is now possible) so that the proportion of the population that can live off the agricultural surplus is very small. The essence of 'development' is the application of power to production and transport, which raises output per man-hour of labour above what human muscle (aided by some animal muscle) can achieve. Thus a programme for development involves a programme for industrialization, which is necessary as much to increase agricultural output as for mining and manufactures.

The attempt to develop is being made under a great

variety of régimes – personal dictatorships, some would-be benevolent, some of the utmost brutality; military juntas; royal dynasties; parliamentary democracies, dating from the nineteenth century or hastily fudged up to take over from an abdicating imperialist power.

The role of the USA in the world today is summed up in an old Soviet joke : 'What is the greatest problem facing the President of the United States – Is it possible to have capitalism in one country?' Every new nationalist movement or reformist political party in the Third World is labelled 'communist' and kept out of power, by force if necessary, so that these régimes (with one or two precarious exceptions), willingly or reluctantly, keep their economies open to trade and investment for the convenience of capitalist business and, in many cases, put their territory and their forces at the disposal of US strategy. The Cuban revolution succeeded in escaping and was obliged to throw itself upon the support of the Soviets. The hypothesis that the leadership of any kind of revolt against oppression must be 'communist' at heart thus becomes self-fulfilling.

The obligation to remain within the rules of the game of the world market puts a number of obstacles in the way of development. The first requirement of development is to mobilize an investable surplus. It is against the rules to expropriate landlords and make use of rent. The profits of native industry are largely consumed in supporting a middle-class standard of life. A great part of the profits generated by exploiting the natural resources of these countries accrues to foreign businesses which carried out investment to open up supplies of raw materials for their home markets before native capitalists had arisen to undertake it; a great part, also, of the profits generated in industry, trade and finance accrues to foreign businesses.[1]

[1] See H. W. Singer, 'The Distribution of Gains between Investing and Borrowing Countries', *American Economic Review* (Papers and Proceedings), May 1950. Reprinted in *International Development: Growth and Change*.

To supplement their inadequate savings from home sources, many of these countries are receiving grants and loans under the title of 'aid'. In some very special cases this has succeeded in fostering native capitalism sufficiently to begin to look after itself; in most, it leads to dependence which inhibits growth rather than promotes it; then loan charges mount from year to year; more and more of current aid is being eaten up in paying for aid already received.

The second problem of development is to direct the investment of whatever surplus is available into the channels which will best promote continuing growth.

'Agriculture is the foundation.' The first step out of millenial poverty is to raise output per head of foodstuffs. The lack of an effective land reform is inimical to development not only because it allows the surplus represented by rent to be consumed in idleness, but because it checks the potential increase in output by leaving land under-utilized and with antiquated techniques, discourages the cultivator and often keeps him at such a low level that he cannot put much energy into work even if he had an incentive to do so, and prevents the mobilization of spare-time labour that has proved so effective in China.[2]

In Mexico, and recently in India, there has been an important development of capitalist farming which is producing a surplus and contributing to growth; at the same time it creates a formidable social and political problem, for the mass of the peasantry gets little benefit from it.

Industrial investment, under the rules of the game, is made where there is a market in sight, principally for the sale of consumption goods to the urban population. The extent to which this has been pre-empted by foreign firms has given rise to the expression cocacolonization; but there has also been a development of native capitalism in this field under protection of one sort or another. Import-saving investment sets the spiral of development going up to a certain point. To cut imports saves the earnings from

[2] Cf. Myrdal, *Asian Drama*, Chapter XXII.

exports or aid for investment; further investment in import saving increases resources for investment and so on round. But this process comes to a dead end when a number of inefficient small scale industries have been set up in each country and all available export earnings are required to pay for materials and components to keep them going.

To increase exports is the great desideratum. Many of the animal, mineral and vegetable products developed under imperialism now provide a useful source of export earnings to the newly independent nations. Even when a large part of the profit goes abroad there is still a benefit, for export receipts cover also the wage bill and retained profits. But here too there are narrow limits to the possibilities of growth. When the production of these commodities was being developed they were guided by the prospects of the market in the industrial countries. There were occasional over-shoots, and there was the devastating slump of the thirties, but generally speaking, supply was tailored to demand so as to maintain profitability. Nowadays the national economies that have inherited them are eager to increase their export earnings wherever they can, so that there is a constant pressure to produce, one country or one continent competing with another to get a share of the proceeds. It is in the nature of these markets to be inelastic – that is to say that an increase in supplies offered brings down the price more than proportionately, so that the result is a chronic tendency to create a buyer's market. Since this is by no means inconvenient to the buyers – the industries of the developed nations – the sellers find very little sympathy for their appeals for help to remedy the situation.

Manufactured exports are the next hope. With low wage rates they can be competitive in textiles and other labour-intensive lines of production. When the British were under-selling handicraft producers they were great believers in free trade, but nowadays the developed nations do not want *their* industries to be undersold; the markets open to would-be developing nations are narrowly limited. Even processing of their own raw materials is kept in check by the tariff arrangements which protect processing industries which grew up in the imperialist countries on the basis of colonial raw materials.[3]

The great international corporations which act as buyers of primary products, or set up manufacturing concerns in the territory of the ex-colonial nations, contribute a great deal to their economies. They bring advanced techniques of marketing and production, train labour and subsidiary levels of the technostructure and support the growth of local businesses ancilliary to their own. But the spiral of development cannot be set going in this way. The surplus is largely transmitted out of the country in the form of profits. When there is reinvestment in expanding the business on the spot it makes a contribution to development, but a high price has to be paid for it. The new capital created on the spot is the legal property of the foreign company and has to pay dividends to foreign shareholders.

The international companies, perfectly correctly from their own point of view, arrange their investments around the world and manipulate the flow of production from one centre or another to suit the requirements of their own profitability, not to promote the viability or growth of particular national economies. Moreover they exercise a strong influence, through the policies of the United States and the ex-imperial powers and through the interests of the native capitalists allied to them, to prevent the local government from getting control over the management of its economy through taxation, tariffs or other devices, and (above all) nationalization, so as to keep the country open to the operation of free enterprise. This system has been characterized as neo-colonialism, because it deprives the new national governments of the independence which was granted on paper when they were set up.

'Aid', no doubt, (particularly technical assistance) has done something in particular countries to promote economic

[3] Cf. Singer, loc. cit.

growth and it has certainly contributed to keeping in being régimes that would otherwise have foundered. But it has been accompanied by the enormous anti-aid of fostering 'defence' forces. The quaint idea of arming Pakistan as a bulwark against the Soviet Union imposed upon the Indians (who knew to what destination the arms were to be directed) a heavy burden of military expenditure. When China was promoted to the rank of the main enemy of the free world, the position was reversed and Pakistan felt obliged to expand its military effort to match the armaments being supplied to India. The Soviet Union also joined the game, turning the cynicism of 'peace-loving' capitalist powers against themselves.

In spite of all, there is development going on in the world. Almost everywhere, statistical national income is rising from year to year. The benefit, however, is being very largely nullified by the growth of population. A rapid rate of growth was already taking place in many countries (particularly the Indian sub-continent) during the colonial period, and medical assistance (for instance in stamping out malaria) increased the rate after the war. In spite of some improvement in nutrition and in employment, the absolute number of children growing up hungry and illiterate increases from year to year and many countries seem to be reaching the point where overall average income per head ceases to rise and begins to fall.[4]

Marx quite correctly criticized Malthus' argument as both illogical and reactionary.[5] Unfortunately he drew from this the conclusion that growing numbers are not a menace to well-being. In the Soviet Union the enormous area with natural resources to be developed, and the great losses during the war, made a growth of numbers an object of policy. Combined with Marx's teaching, it became a dogma that family planning is contrary to socialism. However medical abortion was provided as a social service

[4] Myrdal, *Asian Drama*, Chapter XXVII.
[5] Cf. p. 44 above.

(except for a time under Stalin). Both in the Soviet Union and the People's Democracies the urban birth rate has fallen very low.

Chinese authorities at first followed the orthodox teaching but (while always repudiating Malthus) they have for some years been carrying out a campaign for late marriage and small families. Their network of health services and the intimate contact of the administration with every village and every alleyway makes it possible for information and propaganda to penetrate the whole country very rapidly.

In India and Pakistan family planning is now official policy, but there it is not so easy to bring it to the people. In Africa and Latin America national feeling gives rise to suspicion of a doctrine that is being preached by white men and Yankees, and the implication in some of the arguments being used, that it was after all a pity to have stamped out diseases like malaria, naturally exacerbates suspicion.

After twenty wasted years, in spite of the alliance of Catholic and Marxist orthodoxy, articulate world opinion is now very generally in favour of doing everything possible to get birth-rates down. Technical improvements in contraception are on the way; but even when the perfect foolproof and inoffensive method has been found, it will not be easy to get it into universal use. And even if the birth-rate over the world could be sharply cut in the near future, the age composition of the population that has already got itself born would prevent the overall number of adults from ceasing to grow and reproduce themselves for a long time. It would still require the utmost effort in economic development to bring an appreciable rise in the standard of life.

Chinese experience has shown what development requires. To get the whole population engaged with goodwill in the economic effort and to organize employment so that all can contribute; to increase productivity in agriculture so that a surplus can be extracted without the need to use brutal methods; to check inequality so as not to waste resources on unnecessary consumption and undermine morale by generating envy; to raise the general level of health and to institute birth control; to build up the basis of heavy industry so as to be able to modernize production as fast as possible, and meanwhile to encourage handicrafts to mechanize themselves by means of 'intermediate techniques';[6] to spread education and develop self-reliance (at every level from the paddy field to the atomic laboratory) in applying the scientific method of experiment in every activity.

It remains to be seen whether any other prescription will prove successful.

Meanwhile China, with Russia and Japan, illustrates also the enormous inertia of history. Revolutionaries all over the world are drawing inspiration from the Thought of Mao Tse-tung but it will not supply any ready-made formula for application to the great variety of particular situations which history and geography have created for them.

[6] Cf. E. F. Schumacher: 'Intermediate Technology – a new approach to Foreign Aid.' *Advance* April 2, 1967. (University of Manchester Institute of Science and Technology.)

13

FALSE PROPHETS

Looking out upon this menacing scene, the apologists of modern capitalism have lost their self-confidence. They can find nothing better to offer than the doctrine of the lesser evil. 'To defend the bad against the worse'[1] is no inspiration to generous youth. The revolt of the generation growing up in the mid-twentieth century is largely a rejection of the scale of values that is embodied in accepted orthodoxy.

Accepted orthodoxy is very heavily impregnated by the teaching of the economists which, combined with patriotism, makes the 'growth of national income' the aim of policy and the criterion of success. Statistics of the overall total of national income pay no attention to the distribution of consumption between families or to the composition of the flow of goods and services which it measures. The composition of output is very largely determined by what it is profitable for businesses to sell. In the heyday of economic orthodoxy this was presented as the greatest merit of the system – profit depends upon meeting demand, and demand expresses the free choice of the consumer as to how to dispose of his purchasing power. (Purchasing power is admittedly not distributed according to needs but somehow that was not allowed to spoil the argument.)

Economics was described as the study of human behaviour as a relation between ends and scarce means that have alternative uses. The orthodoxy based upon this conception broke down in a spectacular manner in the great slump when the pursuit of profit was failing to make use of a large part of resources for any end at all.

[1] This phrase from C. Day Lewis 'Where are the war poets?' refers to the defence of the British Empire against facism. In many countries nowadays, of which Greece is the latest example, the problem is rather of defending the worse against the less bad.

It is sometimes said the Keynes saved the capitalist system by convincing governments that they have the power and the duty to preserve near-full employment. However that may be, he certainly saved economics. Without him economics in the English-speaking world would have been completely discredited and policy would have become the domain of cranks and empirics.

Yet to a remarkable extent teaching has slipped back into the old grooves. It is true that the doctrine that what is profitable is best has been a good deal modified by social policy in the welfare state. Investment in hospitals and schools is now admitted to be meeting a more important need than investment in motor-car factories; and there is a great deal of discussion of the problems of policy involved in running a near-full employment economy, the management of the national monetary system, the attempt to avoid inflation, the manipulation of exchange rates and the control of the balance of payments in the conditions of the new mercantilism, and so forth.

But the central teaching of academic economics has altered very little. The core of theory is still the exposition of the operation of a perfectly competitive market which ensures the optimum allocation of given resources between alternative uses. The vulgarized economic doctrines that enter into the stream of public opinion still proclaim the beneficient operation of the unimpeded play of the profit motive.

The notion that the pursuit of individual self-interest produces the greatest benefit to society as a whole came into fashion with modern economics itself. Adam Smith's *Inquiry into the Nature and Causes of the Wealth of Nations* set the keynote. Amongst animals, the individual can fend for himself.

'But man has almost constant occasion for the help of his brethren and it is in vain for him to expect it from their benevolence only. He will be more likely to prevail if

he can interest their self-love in his favour, and show them
that it is to their own advantage to do for him what he
requires of them. . . . It is not from the benevolence of the
butcher, the brewer or the baker that we expect our dinner
but from their regard for their own interests.'

The argument of the *Wealth of Nations* still provides
the basis for a rationalization of an exaggerated version
of the doctrines of laissez faire. For Adam Smith laissez
faire was a programme. Living in a system in which
authority attempted to control economic life in accordance
with a view of national interest and the proper order of
society which he saw to be out of line with the growing
'forces of production' of his day, he advocated the removal
of restrictions upon the free play of the market and pre-
dicted that reliance upon the profit motive would lead to
a great increase in the economic surplus. For him the wealth
of nations did not include the standard of life of the
workers; wages were as much a part of the costs of production as the feed of cattle.

The economists of the nineteenth century admitted that
wages were part of the national income, but they did not
sufficiently consider what a radical change in emphasis this
required. Wicksell, indeed, in the introduction to his
Lectures declared :

'As soon as we begin seriously to regard economic
phenomena *as a whole* and to seek for the conditions of
the welfare of the whole, consideration for the interests of
the proletariat must emerge; and from thence to the
proclamation of *equal* rights for all is only a short step.

'The very concept of political economy, therefore, or the
existence of a science with such a name, implies, strictly
speaking, a thoroughly revolutionary programme.'

But his own treatment of economic theory did nothing to
undermine the presumption that profitability is the proper
guide for production.

Marshall, also, could not accept the ruthless amorality of pure laissez faire but he salved his conscience with the need for 'the strongest, and not merely the highest, forces of human nature' to be utilized for the social good; that is, when it came to the point, he endorsed the view that self-interest and public duty coincide.

There is an obvious fallacy in this doctrine. If the pursuit of profit is the criterion of proper behaviour there is no way of distinguishing between productive activity and robbery. Claud Cockburn recounts how he had an interview with the 'millionaire murderer' Al Capone. When Cockburn made some sympathetic remark about the hard conditions of childhood in the slums of Brooklyn, Capone was upset.

' "Listen," he said, "don't get the idea I'm one of these goddam radicals. Don't get the idea I'm knocking the American system. The American system—" As though an invisible chairman had called upon him for a few words, he broke into an oration upon the theme. He praised freedom, enterprise and the pioneers. He spoke of "our heritage". He referred with contemptuous disgust to Socialism and Anarchism. "My rackets," he repeated several times, "are run on strictly American lines and they're going to stay that way.

*   *   *

' "This American system of ours," he shouted, "call it Americanism, call it Capitalism, call it what you like, gives to each and every one of us a great opportunity if we only seize it with both hands and make the most of it." '[2]

To draw an arbitrary line by law and impose it by force is both expensive and ineffective. The laissez faire system which was good for accumulation at all costs does not provide any guidance for enjoying the fruits; indeed, its cult of self-interest and competition has created the lonely

[2] Cockburn, *I, Claud*, p. 118–9 (Penguin Edition).

crowd of other-directed status-seekers which the social scientists find far from satisfactory.

When Keynes first realized the possibilities of continuous accumulation, he conceived that ('assuming no important wars and no important increase in population') the economic problem might be finally solved.

'Now it is true that the needs of human beings may seem to be insatiable. But they fall into two classes – those needs which are absolute in the sense that we feel them whatever the situation of our fellow human beings may be, and those which are relative in the sense that we feel them only if their satisfaction lifts us above, makes us feel superior to, our fellows. Needs of the second class, those which satisfy the desire for superiority, may indeed be insatiable; for the higher the general level, the higher still are they. But this is not so true of the absolute needs – a point may soon be reached, much sooner perhaps than we are all of us aware of, when these needs are satisfied in the sense that we prefer to devote our further energies to non-economic purposes.

* * *

'I see us free, therefore, to return to some of the most sure and certain principles of religion and traditional virtue – that avarice is a vice, that the exaction of usury is a misdemeanour, and the love of money is detestable, that those walk most truly in the paths of virtue and sane wisdom who take least thought for the morrow. We shall once more value ends above means and prefer the good to the useful. We shall honour those who can teach us how to pluck the hour and the day virtuously and well, the delightful people who are capable of taking direct enjoyment in things, the lilies of the field who toil not, neither do they spin.'[3]

In spite of both wars and population growth, capitalism with near-full employment has succeeded in producing a

[3] Keynes, 'Economic Possibilities for our Grandchildren', *Essays in Persuasion*, p. 358 et seq.

level of consumption per head undreamed of in former ages, but the change in our sense of values that Keynes was pleading for is not in evidence. On the contrary, commercial considerations swallow up more and more of social life, so that those who want to demand, say, improvements in the health service find it politic to point to the loss of production due to sickness and those who are concerned with education evaluate its benefits in terms of the salaries of trained personnel.

In Europe the commercial system grew up within the framework of an aristocracy. From one point of view the notion of status based on wealth acquired, not inherited, was democratic – a protest against 'birth'. Transplanted to the United States, without the shell of aristocratic traditions, it grew and flourished mightily; it now comes back to reign not only in Western Europe but also in the native capitalism that grew up under the shelter of the European empires, so that 'freedom' has come to be identified with freedom to make money. (But in the United States itself the caricature of aristocracy installed in the slave states has left an awkward legacy.)

14

SCIENCE AND MORALITY

THE ever-growing intellectual curiosity of modern man makes mankind itself an object of study. Modern science, which began with what is most remote from us – astronomy – now seeks to plot the mechanisms of individual personality and to find out the laws governing social behaviour. The great prestige of the natural sciences and the spectacular technology founded upon them leads to the hope that if only scientific method could be applied to the study of society we might hope to find a solution for the dreadful problems hanging over our life today.

There is not yet much reason to expect that such a grand programme can be fulfilled. The methods to which the natural sciences owe their success – controlled experiment and exact observation of continually recurring phenomena – cannot be applied to the study of human beings by human beings. So far, no equally successful method of establishing reliable natural laws has been suggested.

Certainly, the social sciences should not be unscientific. Their practitioners should not jump to conclusions on inadequate evidence or propound circular statements that are true by definition as though they had some factual content; when they disagree they should not resort to abuse like theologians or literary critics, but should calmly set about to investigate the nature of the difference and to propose a plan of research to resolve it.

Norbert Wiener comments upon the use in theoretical economics of the mathematics appropriate to classical physics.

'The success of mathematical physics led the social scientist to be jealous of its power without quite understanding the intellectual attitudes that had contributed to this power. The use of mathematical formulae had accompanied the development of the natural sciences and become the mode in the social sciences. Just as primitive peoples adopt the Western modes of denationalized clothing and of parliamentarism out of a vague feeling that these magic rites and vestments will at once put them abreast of modern culture and technique, so the economists have developed the habit of dressing up their rather imprecise ideas in the language of the infinitesimal calculus.'[1]

Nowadays the pretensions of the economists have impressed some of the exponents of other branches of social studies, who are aping the economists aping the physicists. Others, revolted by the spectacle, reject economics altogether and try to explain society by psychological principles alone.

But even if the social scientists could improve their methodologies and raise their level of intellectual discipline, it would not be possible for them to provide a basis for 'social engineering' comparable to that which the physicists have provided for space engineering. The reason is obvious. The objective of an engineering programme is given to the engineer; for the social scientist the objective of the programme is precisely what he has to discuss. It is of no use to explain people to themselves as though they were automata. 'Every man hath business and desire.' The scientist cannot set himself up as a superior being who is exempt from the operation of the laws that he is expounding. The readers can retort to the writer – if we are automata, what are you?

The function of social science is quite different from that of the natural sciences – it is to provide society with an organ of self-consciousness.

Every interconnected group of human beings has to have an ideology – that is, a conception of what is the proper way to behave and the permissible pattern of relationships in family, economic and political life. Even the apes have

[1] Wiener, *God and Golem Inc.*, p. 91.

a conception of what is 'not done'. The mother chimpanzee pulls the toddler away when she catches him playing with a baboon.

For humans, emancipated from set instincts, ideologies are highly malleable. There is an analogy, which is more than a metaphor, between the capacity to learn language and the capacity to learn a code of proper behaviour.[2] The human brain evidently contains an apparatus that allows a child to master not only a vocabulary but the rules of no matter how complicated a grammatical structure, without directing conscious effort to the task. (It would be a great convenience if a hormone could be found that would keep this ability alive in later life.) The ability is common to humanity, but what language a child learns depends upon the community into which he is born.[3] Similarly there is a capacity, no less indispensable to social life, to develop a conscience, or sense of moral values, while the content of the code varies widely from one community to another or from one class to another within a community. (For criminal gangs, strict observance of their code is even more vital than for honest householders; the police would be helpless if they could not sometimes corrupt informers.) It is much easier to learn a language than to learn a code of moral values and the criteria of correctness in grammar for any one language are more precise than the criteria for the validity of ethical principles. In each group what can and what cannot be done is painfully learned by successive generations. This is clearly seen in the most basic requirement of social organization – a code regulating the relations of the sexes. In every age, in every tribe and nation, the young of each generation have been tormented by the arbitrary rules imposed upon them by the traditions

[2] Cf. Joan Robinson, *Economic Philosophy*, pp. 8–11.

[3] See Naom Chomsky, 'Current Issues in Linguistic Theory', in *The Structure of Language*, ed. Jerry A. Fodor and Jerrold J. Katz, for a review of this position. See also Eric H. Lenneberg, 'The Capacity for Language Acquisition' in the same volume.

in which their elders have felt obliged to bring them up.

Pre-scientific explanations of society in terms of religion, history and 'race' have played a very important part in building up ideology, keeping society in order and fostering patriotism to strengthen one people against another. This was social self-consciousness at, so they say, the first degree.

The task of social science now is to raise self-consciousness to the second degree, to find out the causes, the mode of functioning and the consequences of the adoption of ideologies, so as to submit them to rational criticism. Only too often would-be scientists are still operating at the first degree, propagating some ideology which serves some particular interest, as the economists' doctrine of laissez faire served the interest of capitalist business.

There has been a good deal of confused controversy about the question of 'value judgments' in the social sciences. Every human being has ideological, moral and political views. To pretend to have none and to be *purely objective* must necessarily be either self-deception or a device to deceive others. A candid writer will make his preconceptions clear and allow the reader to discount them if he does not accept them. This concerns the professional honour of the scientist. But to eliminate value judgments from the subject-matter of social science is to eliminate the subject itself, for since it concerns human behaviour it must be concerned with the value judgments that people make. The social scientist (whatever he may privately believe) has no right to pretend to know any better than his neighbours what ends society should serve. His business is to show them why they believe what they purport to believe (as far as he can make it out) and what influence beliefs have on behaviour.

But just as there are some basic elements which set limits to the possible structures of languages[4] so there is a core of common values in all moral codes. Our brains refuse

[4] ibid,

to conceive of a language without, in some form or another, a distinction between nouns and verbs to reflect the distinction between objects and actions; equally our brains refuse to admit the possibility of a society which, for instance, admires cowardice (though it may value prudence), or that prefers cruelty to kindness within its own kind. If we add to this the principle that the morality is to be preferred that has the widest inclusiveness, we have a sufficient basis for the formulation of moral judgments of moral systems.

A black man may know from personal experience that white racism is cruel and obscene, or an unemployed man that the economic system is harsh and arbitrary. It is not unscientific for an observer of society to use those adjectives in the course of description or analysis (provided that adjectives are not merely a substitute for observation). It is not impossible for honest men to understand each other even when their ideas were formed in totally different traditions.

A social scientist who acknowledges that his subject is involved in human values, is apt to be too optimistic about the practical influence that he can exert, for the group interests that group ideologies defend are not easily to be reconciled by his general principle.

Very likely, since he has a professional commitment to faith in the power of reason and has, on the whole, a humane sense of values, he expects that, when people in general can see the problem as he expounds it, they will want to act as he believes they should. Keynes maintained that when the operation of the capitalist system is understood, its great productive power would be used to abolish poverty and create conditions in which we would 'prefer to devote our further energies to non-economic purposes'. Myrdal argued in his *American Dilemma* that, by exposing the mythology of race, reason would erode colour prejudice and so help to establish a régime of equality before the law in the Southern States of USA. Both these hopes are still a long way from fulfilment.

This does not mean that it was of no use to find out the causes of unemployment or to present the situation of the blacks as a dilemma for the white Americans who pretend to believe in democracy.

Anyone who writes a book, however gloomy its message may be, is necessarily an optimist. If the pessimists really believed what they were saying there would be no point in saying it.

The economists of the laissez-faire school purported to abolish the moral problem by showing that the pursuit of self-interest by each individual rebounds to the benefit of all. The task of the generation now in rebellion is to reassert the authority of morality over technology; the business of social scientists is to help them to see both how necessary and how difficult that task is going to be.

INDEX OF SOURCES

SUBJECT INDEX

JOAN ROBINSON, the world-renowned professor of economics at Cambridge University, has played a major role in shaping economic theory in this century. Among her books are *The Economics of Imperfect Competition, Essays in the Theory of Employment, Introduction to the Theory of Employment, Private Enterprise or Public Control, The Problem of Full Employment, The Future of Industry, The Accumulation of Capital, Economic Philosophy, The New Mercantilism,* as well as *Economics: An Awkward Corner.*

Professor Robinson has taught at universities throughout the world. She is married to E. A. G. Robinson and is the mother of two daughters.